Morality
Life in Christ

faith first

Legacy Edition

RCL Benziger®

Cincinnati, Ohio

This book reflects the
new revision of the

ROMAN
MISSAL
THIRD EDITION

"The Ad Hoc Committee to Oversee the Use of the Catechism, United States Conference of Catholic Bishops, has found this catechetical series, copyright 2006, to be in conformity with the *Catechism of the Catholic Church*."

NIHIL OBSTAT
Rev. Msgr. Robert M. Coerver
Censor Librorum

IMPRIMATUR
† Most Rev. Charles V. Grahmann
Bishop of Dallas

September 1, 2004

The Nihil Obstat and Imprimatur are official declarations that the material reviewed is free of doctrinal or moral error. No implication is contained therein that those granting the Nihil Obstat and Imprimatur agree with the contents, opinions, or statements expressed.

Send all inquiries to:
RCL Benziger
8805 Governor's Hill Drive
Suite 400
Cincinnati, Ohio 45249

Toll Free 877-275-4725
Fax   800-688-8356

Visit us at **www.RCLBenziger.com**
          www.FaithFirst.com

20478   ISBN 978-0-7829-1071-1 (Student Book)
20498   ISBN 978-0-7829-1083-4 (Catechist Guide)
20529   ISBN 978-0-7829-1114-5 (Teacher Guide)

Manufactured for RCL Benziger in Cincinnati, OH, USA.

ACKNOWLEDGMENTS

Scripture excerpts are taken or adapted from the *New American Bible with Revised New Testament and Psalms* Copyright © 1991, 1986, 1970, Confraternity of Christian Doctrine, Washington, D.C. Used with permission. All rights reserved. No part of the *New American Bible* may be reproduced by any means without the permission of the copyright owner.

Excerpts are taken or adapted from the English translation of the *Roman Missal* © 2010, International Commission on English in the Liturgy, Inc. (ICEL); the English translation of *Rite of Penance* © 1974, ICEL; the English translation of *A Book of Prayers* © 1982, ICEL; the English translation of *A Book of Blessings* © 1988, ICEL; *Catholic Household Blessings and Prayers* (revised edition) © 2007, United States Conference of Catholic Bishops, Washington, D.C. All rights reserved.

Excerpts are taken or adapted from the English translation of *Kyrie Eleison, Nicene Creed, Apostles' Creed, Sanctus and Benedictus, Agnus Dei, Gloria Patri,* and *Te Deum Laudamus* by the International Consultation on English Texts (ICET).

Faith First Legacy Edition Development Team

Developing a religion program requires the gifts and talents of many individuals working together as a team. RCL Benziger is proud to acknowledge the contributions of these dedicated people.

Program Theology Consultants
Reverend Louis J. Cameli, S.T.D.
Reverend Robert D. Duggan, S.T.D.

Advisory Board
Judith Deckers, M.Ed.
Marina Herrera, Ph.D.
Elaine McCarron, SCN, M.Div.
Reverend Frank McNulty, S.T.D.
Reverend Ronald J. Nuzzi, Ph.D.

National Catechetical Advisor
Jacquie Jambor

Catechetical Specialist
Jo Rotunno

Contributing Writers
Student Book and Catechist/Teacher Guides
Christina DeCamp
Judith Deckers
Reverend Robert D. Duggan
Mary Beth Jambor
Reverend Steven M. Lanza
Eileen A. McGrath
Michele Norfleet

Art and Design Director	*Electronic Page Makeup*	*Production Director*
Lisa Brent	Laura Fremder	Jenna Nelson

Designers/Photo Research	*Project Editors*	*Web Site Producers*
Pat Bracken	Patricia A. Classick	Joseph Crisalli
Kristy O. Howard	Steven M. Ellair	Demere Henson
Susan Smith	Ronald C. Lamping	

General Editor	*President/Publisher*
Ed DeStefano	Maryann Nead

Contents

Welcome to Faith First

Welcome to **Faith First—Morality: Life in Christ!** You are about to begin an exploration of the principles of Catholic morality. Morality deals with the principles that affect the choices we make day by day to live as Catholics. In the weeks ahead you will learn more about your call to holiness as a person created in God's own image. You will learn how the Beatitudes and the Ten Commandments provide foundations for successful moral living. Above all, you will learn more about the model for the moral life, Jesus Christ, and what it means to live in Christ. In him you will find a perfect blueprint for combining love of God and neighbor in a life that balances prayer with action. Throughout, you will discover how the Holy Spirit inspires and empowers you to grow and develop as a moral person.

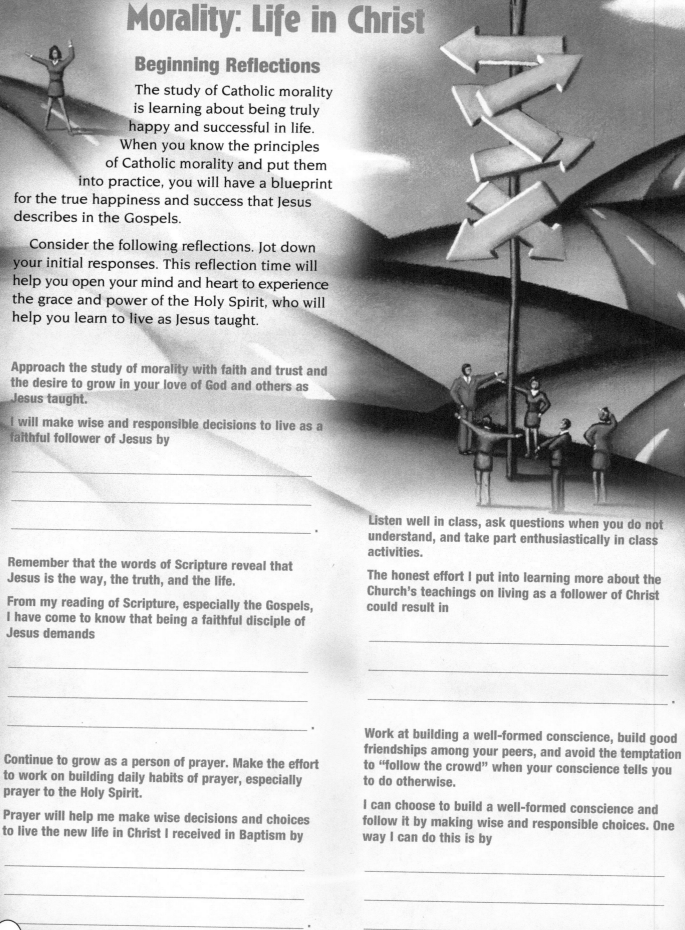

Morality: Life in Christ

Beginning Reflections

The study of Catholic morality is learning about being truly happy and successful in life. When you know the principles of Catholic morality and put them into practice, you will have a blueprint for the true happiness and success that Jesus describes in the Gospels.

Consider the following reflections. Jot down your initial responses. This reflection time will help you open your mind and heart to experience the grace and power of the Holy Spirit, who will help you learn to live as Jesus taught.

Approach the study of morality with faith and trust and the desire to grow in your love of God and others as Jesus taught.

I will make wise and responsible decisions to live as a faithful follower of Jesus by

_____

_____

_____ .

Remember that the words of Scripture reveal that Jesus is the way, the truth, and the life.

From my reading of Scripture, especially the Gospels, I have come to know that being a faithful disciple of Jesus demands

_____

_____

_____ .

Continue to grow as a person of prayer. Make the effort to work on building daily habits of prayer, especially prayer to the Holy Spirit.

Prayer will help me make wise decisions and choices to live the new life in Christ I received in Baptism by

_____

_____ .

Listen well in class, ask questions when you do not understand, and take part enthusiastically in class activities.

The honest effort I put into learning more about the Church's teachings on living as a follower of Christ could result in

_____

_____ .

Work at building a well-formed conscience, build good friendships among your peers, and avoid the temptation to "follow the crowd" when your conscience tells you to do otherwise.

I can choose to build a well-formed conscience and follow it by making wise and responsible choices. One way I can do this is by

_____

_____ .

UNIT ONE
Life in Christ

EXECUTE JUSTICE NOT PEOPLE

What is the connection between holiness and happiness?

Getting Ready

Beatitudes

What do you already know about the Beatitudes?

_____

_____

_____

_____

_____

_____

_____

_____

_____

Questions I Have

What questions about the Beatitudes do you hope these chapters will answer?

_____

_____

_____

_____

_____

Faith Vocabulary

Put an X next to the faith vocabulary terms that you know. Put a ? next to the faith vocabulary terms that you need to know more about.

_____ holiness

_____ soul

_____ Evangelist

_____ disciple

_____ morality

_____ natural law

_____ conscience

_____ evangelize

_____ moral virtues

_____ theological virtues

_____ grace

_____ sanctifying grace

A Scripture Story

The rich man who went away sad

What does it mean to live in Christ?

Human Dignity and Happiness

FAITH FOCUS

What is true happiness?

FAITH VOCABULARY

sanctifying grace
soul
free will
Beatitudes

holiness
intellect
actual grace

What brings you happiness?

Holiness and *happiness* are two words that often are misunderstood. Many people choose paths to happiness that end up bringing them just the opposite.

What is the connection between our search for happiness and our living holy lives?

The LORD called me from birth, . . . he gave me my name.
ISAIAH 49:1

God's Gift to Everyone—Without Exception

Awe and wonder, which are two of the Gifts of the Holy Spirit, give us the vision to see the beauty and holiness of human life. God values each of us as his treasured child. Through Isaiah the Prophet, God says:

> Can a mother forget her infant,
> be without tenderness
> for the child of her womb?
> Even should she forget,
> I will never forget you.
> See, upon the palms of my hands
> I have written your name.
>
> ISAIAH 49:15–16

We are children of God created in his own image and likeness (see Genesis 1:27). God shares his life with everyone—without exception. This is why every human being is sacred, or holy.

We call this gift of God sharing his life and love with us **sanctifying grace.** Sanctifying grace makes us holy, or one with God. Sanctifying grace is our own personal participation in the life of the Trinity. The fact that God dwells in us and with us is the foundation of our dignity as human beings.

Why is every human life sacred?

Baptized into the Life of Christ

God shares the gift of his life and love with us. At the same time, God gives us the freedom to choose whether we will accept his gift or reject it.

The story of the Fall (see Genesis 3:1–24) tells us about the rejection of God's gift of a life with him. After the Fall, God did not let things stand as they were. He promised to send a savior to restore our life in him. Jesus Christ, the Incarnate Son of God, is the Savior God promised.

At Baptism we are joined to Christ and our life with God the Holy Trinity is restored. We receive the new life of **holiness** in Christ and the gift of the Holy Spirit, the third divine Person of the Trinity. Holiness is living our life in Christ.

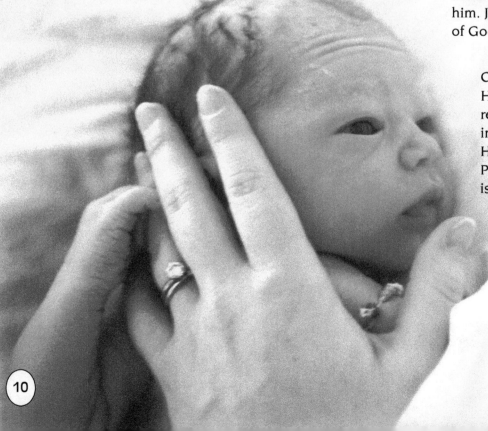

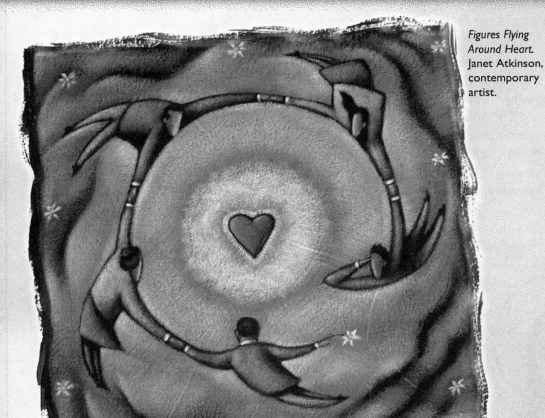

Figures Flying Around Heart. Janet Atkinson, contemporary artist.

A pilgrimage is a journey to a sacred place. The life of a Christian has also been described as a pilgrimage. We are pilgrims on an earthly journey toward the kingdom of God. One way Christians throughout the ages have outwardly expressed they were on a spiritual journey was by making a pilgrimage. Heading toward a destination of true happiness with God was reflected in traveling to a sacred or holy place. Christians still do this today as they make pilgrimages to Rome or the Holy Land or other shrines that celebrate the mysteries of our faith.

Seeking and Finding Happiness

From the moment of our conception, we are destined to enjoy life with God—and with one another—forever. This is the very reason God created us.

God has created human beings with a body and a **soul.** Our soul is spiritual and immortal. It never dies. God has also blessed us with the gifts of an **intellect** and a **free will.** The gift of our intellect is the power to know God and to reflect on how God is part of our lives. The gift of free will is the ability to love and serve God and to choose to center our lives around him.

We will only be happy when we work toward doing just that. When we try to love God and our neighbors, we are cooperating with God's grace. We are showing our respect for the sacredness of life. We are traveling the road to true happiness—a happiness that will last forever.

FAITH CONNECTION

Complete the sentence "Happiness is . . .". Then describe how choosing to live a life of holiness can lead to that happiness.

Happiness

Happiness is _____

_____

_____.

Holiness

_____

_____

_____.

Holiness: Our True Calling

People travel different roads in their search for happiness. Fifteen-year-old Thérèse Martin entered the Carmelite convent in France. From that day on she dreamed of doing great things for God. The years passed without her dream being remotely realized. Naturally, she was disappointed. Then one day she was reading Saint Paul, where he says the best way to holiness is not doing great things for God but doing loving things (see 1 Corinthians 12:31–13:13). After reading this passage, she wrote in her journal: "O Jesus, . . . at last I have found my calling: my calling is love."

Thérèse was summarizing what Jesus taught when he was asked, "Teacher, which commandment in the law is the greatest?" (Matthew 22:36). Jesus said:

"You shall love the Lord, your God, with all your heart, with all your soul, and with all your mind. This is the greatest and the first commandment. The second is like it: You shall love your neighbor as yourself. The whole law and the prophets depend on these two commandments."

MATTHEW 22:37–40

Today we know Thérèse Martin (1873–1897) as Saint Thérèse of Lisieux. In 1997 Pope John Paul II named her "Doctor of the Church." Thérèse, in her own way, was describing the way to holiness. In both words and actions we are to love God with our whole heart, soul, and mind, and to love our neighbor as ourselves. We are to do loving things.

Holiness and Happiness

Today the journey to happiness many people travel is often out of control. Some try to find happiness in fast cars, fine food, drugs, fashions, sex, money, or the accumulation of possessions. Like a car speeding out of control on the interstate, they leave behind a legacy of broken dreams and shattered lives—including their own. Saint Augustine of Hippo (354–430) once made that ill-fated search. After traveling too many dead-end roads, he came to his senses and discovered that God alone is the source of true and lasting human happiness.

By choosing God first and keeping God first, we too will be satisfied. We will realize that striving for holiness and searching for happiness are not opposites—provided we are searching for true happiness.

What are some examples of loving actions that can lead to greater holiness?

Saint Thérèse of Lisieux

Jesus Is Our Model

Jesus is our model for living a holy and happy life. During his life on earth Jesus showed us ways to love God and others—even when he was ridiculed and persecuted. He taught his disciples the principle of holiness and happiness:

"I give you a new commandment: love one another. As I have loved you, so you also should love one another."   JOHN 13:34

The Holy Spirit Is Our Guide and Helper

It is not as though God left us on our own to figure out how to live our life in Christ. No, God the Father pours out the Holy Spirit upon us. The Holy Spirit constantly energizes us, directs us, and strengthens us to respond to the divine invitation to seek happiness by living holy lives. This help is called **actual grace**. Actual grace comes in many forms. It is divine help empowering us to live as adopted daughters and sons of God the Father.

The Church Is Our Mother and Teacher

We do not search for happiness and holiness alone. We are members of the new People of God, the Church. Through the gift and guidance of the Church and the celebration of the sacraments, we are joined with Christ and one another.

Describe the ways the Church can help us in our search for holiness and happiness.

Teenagers and adults building a Habitat for Humanity home

The Beatitudes

Jesus taught about the practical connection between happiness and holiness in the **Beatitudes.** The Beatitudes identify the people and actions blessed by God. They describe the happiness, or blessedness, of those people who keep their lives focused and centered on God and do loving things.

Here are the Beatitudes Jesus taught:

"Blessed are the poor in spirit,
    for theirs is the kingdom
        of heaven.
Blessed are they who mourn,
    for they will be comforted.
Blessed are the meek,
    for they will inherit the land.
Blessed are they who hunger and
        thirst for righteousness,
    for they will be satisfied.
Blessed are the merciful,
    for they will be shown mercy.
Blessed are the clean of heart,
    for they will see God.
Blessed are the peacemakers,
    for they will be called children
        of God.
Blessed are they who are
        persecuted for the sake
        of righteousness,
    for theirs is the kingdom
        of heaven." MATTHEW 5:3–10

The Beatitudes are a summary of the heart of Jesus' teachings on discipleship. They direct our attention toward the kingdom of God—our eternal life of happiness and holiness. To reach that goal we follow the way Jesus pointed out to us by his own teachings and the example of his life.

FAITH CONNECTION

Reread the Beatitudes. Think about the connection between the Beatitudes and happiness and holiness. How might you try to live one of the Beatitudes this week?

_____

_____

_____

OUR CHURCH MAKES A DIFFERENCE

Respect Life

Jesus came to bring life—and to help us live life to the fullest. The Catholic Church has constantly reaffirmed that all life is a wonderful and precious gift from God. The Respect Life Program of the United States Conference of Catholic Bishops (USCCB) is one way the Church keeps before our eyes the importance of respecting the sacredness of all life. The United States Conference of Catholic Bishops, through its pro-life activities, helps all people fulfill their responsibilities to respect the sacredness of human life at every stage of its existence.

Cardinal Joseph Bernardin speaking to worshipers at St. Barbara Church, Brookfield, Illinois

Cardinal Joseph Bernardin (1928–1996), Archbishop of Chicago, reminded Catholics in 1983 that respect for life means respect for all life. He used the image of a "seamless garment" to teach vividly that every single human life is important and that our work on behalf of the unborn, disabled, elderly, and dying cannot be separated one from the other.

What do you do each day that shows your respect and reverence for all human life?

WHAT DIFFERENCE

Does Faith Make in My Life?

Choose Life

All life is a sacred gift from God. Human life is present from the moment a baby is conceived. From the moment of conception to a person's death, life is to be cared for and treasured.

Our Society

Look around your world and listen to the teachings of our society. You will hear many messages that are contrary to the sacredness of life. Many people express opinions, make choices, and act in a way that harms or destroys life. But as human beings and Catholics, you are called to always choose life.

Our Church

To be a follower of Christ and a member of the Church, you will be asked to go against some popular opinions about the sacredness of life. This could be very uncomfortable. It may cause you some suffering and it is definitely unpopular.

The Catholic Church speaks out and asks you to speak out about the sacredness of *all* life. Based on the teaching of the Catholic Church, what would you say about the morality of one of these issues? Provide reasons for your answers.

- ◆ **Capital punishment**—the government's right to put a prisoner to death

- ◆ **Abortion**—a woman's right to end the life of her unborn child

- ◆ **Assisted suicide**—a sick or elderly person's right to have someone help them end their own life

Death penalty opponents holding a prayer vigil outside Washington State Penitentiary

Pro-life marchers outside Supreme Court building, Washington, D.C.

There are so many other difficult questions you will be asked to think about as our society continues to make choices that are not in favor of life. As members of the Catholic Church, we must always choose life. That means we respect and accept the dignity of every human being from conception to death.

Faith • • Decision

- Form a small group and discuss how you can speak out in favor of life as a sacred gift from God.

- Using art, music, or role-play, illustrate what you have discussed.

This week I can continue to choose life by

_____

_____

_____

_____.

The Beatitudes

Leader: In the Beatitudes Jesus gives us both a vision and practical guidelines to seek and find happiness by living holy lives. Let us open our hearts and minds in prayer.

All: **Jesus, you are the way to holiness and happiness.**

Reader 1: "Blessed are the poor in spirit, for theirs is the kingdom of heaven.

All: **Jesus, . . .**

Reader 2: Blessed are they who mourn, for they will be comforted.

All: **Jesus, . . .**

Reader 3: Blessed are the meek, for they will inherit the land.

All: **Jesus, . . .**

Reader 4: Blessed are they who hunger and thirst for righteousness, for they will be satisfied.

All: **Jesus, . . .**

Reader 5: Blessed are the merciful, for they will be shown mercy.

All: **Jesus, . . .**

Reader 6: Blessed are the clean of heart, for they will see God.

All: **Jesus, . . .**

Reader 7: Blessed are the peacemakers, for they will be called children of God.

All: **Jesus, . . .**

Reader 8: Blessed are they who are persecuted for the sake of righteousness, for theirs is the kingdom of heaven."

MATTHEW 5:3–12

Leader: Lord Jesus, you are the way, the truth, and the life. Guide us in living as you taught so we may rejoice with you, the Father, and the Holy Spirit forever in eternal happiness.

All: **Amen.**

FAITH VOCABULARY

Define each of these terms:

1. sanctifying grace
2. holiness
3. soul
4. intellect
5. free will
6. actual grace
7. Beatitudes

MAIN IDEAS

Choose either (a) or (b) from each set of items. Write a brief paragraph to answer each of your choices.

1. (a) What does it mean to say that every human being without exception is sacred, or holy?

   (b) Describe the Christian understanding of holiness.

2. (a) Describe the connection between searching for happiness and striving to live a holy life.

   (b) How do the Beatitudes guide us in our search for true happiness?

CRITICAL THINKING

Using what you have learned in this chapter, briefly explain this statement:
   We are called to a fullness of life which far exceeds our life on earth.

FAMILY DISCUSSION

What is it that truly makes our family happy? How does that happiness compare with the happiness that Jesus taught?

For more ideas on ways your family can live your faith, visit the "Faith First for Families" page at **www.FaithFirst.com**. Also check out "Make a Difference" on the Teen Center.

One Person's Decision

A Scripture Story

FAITH FOCUS

How does learning about Saint Mark the Evangelist help us understand the Gospel?

FAITH VOCABULARY

Evangelists

Who helps you make decisions?

We turn to many people for advice when we are faced with making important decisions. Many people came to ask Jesus' advice when they had questions about their lives. We too are faced with making decisions each day about how we are to live as followers of Jesus. We can find answers to many of our questions in the Scriptures.

How can reading the Gospels help you make decisions about life?

Depiction of Jesus and the rich man (Mark 10:17–31), stained glass

"Go, sell what you have, and give to [the] poor and you will have treasure in heaven; then come, follow me."

MARK 10:21

Bible Background

The Evangelists

After Jesus died and ascended to his Father, the Apostles became proclaimers of the Gospel. They traveled around telling everyone about the life-death-Resurrection-Ascension and teachings of Jesus. Eventually, the teachings of the Apostles about Jesus began to be written down. This enabled the Church to preserve the authentic teachings of the Apostles for all ages.

The inspired writers of the Gospel are called **Evangelists**, or "Tellers of the Good News." The Church recognizes four written accounts of the Gospel as inspired by God. The Gospels of Matthew, Mark, Luke, and John are the first four books of the New Testament.

Inspired by the Holy Spirit, each of the four Evangelists authentically presented the Gospel. Each Evangelist wrote his account of the Gospel to bring others to faith in God the Father through his Son, Jesus, with the help of the Holy Spirit. Each Evangelist took a slightly different path to get this message across to his listeners and readers. Understanding the writing style and technique of each Evangelist can help us understand and enjoy the message of each account of the Gospel.

What might have happened if the Gospel stories of Jesus had not been written?

Details from *Christ and the Four Evangelists*, stained-glass window. Henry Holiday (1839–1927), British artist.

Saint Mark the Evangelist is often depicted by Christian artists as writing his account of the Gospel with a winged lion near his side. The image of a winged lion comes from Mark 1:3. In this passage Mark describes John the Baptist as "[a] voice of one crying out in the desert." Christian artists used the idea of a roaring lion to capture the meaning of this passage. The wings come from the prophet Ezekiel's vision of four winged living creatures (see Ezekiel 10:20–21), which Christians have come to identify with the four Evangelists.

View of Ancient Rome. Antonio Basali (1774–1848), Italian artist and theater designer.

The Gospel According to Mark

The Gospel according to Mark was written sometime after A.D. 64 and before the destruction of the Temple in Jerusalem in A.D. 70. Saint Mark's Gospel was written to Gentile, or non-Jewish, followers of Christ living in Rome.

Mark tells the story of Jesus in a fast-paced style, describing Jesus moving rapidly from one place to another to preach. There is a definite urgency to Mark's message.

The Christians in Rome for whom Mark wrote were being persecuted because of their faith. Mark's Gospel was a powerful source of comfort and a call to faith for these Christians.

FAITH CONNECTION

Look up and read these Gospel passages. Summarize how Jesus' teaching in each passage is a source of courage for Christians to live their faith in Christ. Discuss your reflections with a partner.

Mark 8:34–37 | Mark 9:30–32

Reading the Word of God

Rich Man Who Went Away Sorrowful.
James J. Tissot (1836–1902), French painter.

"Come, Follow Me!"

Making decisions is part of everyone's day. Some decisions are more important than others. Some are easier to make than others. Saint Mark the Evangelist calls his listeners and readers to make the decision to follow Christ.

Saint Mark vividly drives home this point in his story about the wealthy young man who asked Jesus, "Good teacher, what must I do to inherit eternal life?" (Mark 10:17). Jesus answered him,

"You know the commandments: 'You shall not kill; you shall not commit adultery; you shall not steal; you shall not bear false witness; you shall not defraud; honor your father and your mother.'" He replied and said to him, "Teacher, all of these I have observed from my youth." Jesus, looking at him, loved him and said to him, "You are lacking in one thing. Go, sell what you have, and give to [the] poor and you will have treasure in heaven; then come, follow me." At that statement his face fell, and he went away sad, for he had many possessions.

Jesus looked around and said to his disciples, "How hard it is for those who have wealth to enter the kingdom of God!" The disciples were amazed at his words. So Jesus again said to them in reply, "Children, how hard it is to enter the kingdom of God! It is easier for a camel to pass through [the] eye of [a] needle than for one who is rich to enter the kingdom of God." They were exceedingly astonished and said among themselves, "Then who can be saved?" Jesus looked at them and said, "For human beings it is impossible, but not for God. All things are possible for God." Peter began to say to him, "We have given up everything and followed you." Jesus said, "Amen, I say to you, there is no one who has given up house or brothers or sisters or mother or father or children or lands for my sake and for the sake of the gospel who will not receive a hundred times more now in this present age: . . . eternal life in the age to come. But many that are first will be last, and [the] last will be first."

MARK 10:18–31

Jesus invited the wealthy young man to follow him. By making the decision to follow Jesus, the young man would find the happiness, eternal life, for which he was searching—that perhaps his wealth was not bringing him. The young man was not ready to make that decision.

Describe the wealthy young man's response to Jesus. In what way is the young man's response similar to what yours would be? Unlike yours?

Did you Know...

The first disciples chosen by Jesus are also called the Twelve. They are "Simon called Peter, and his brother Andrew; James, the son of Zebedee, and his brother John; Philip and Bartholomew, Thomas and Matthew the tax collector; James, the son of Alphaeus, and Thaddeus; Simon the Cananean, and Judas Iscariot who betrayed him" (Matthew 10:2–4).

The Cost of Being a Disciple of Jesus

Saint Mark devotes a whole section, chapters 9 through 15, of his brief Gospel to being a disciple of Jesus. He paints a very vivid and detailed picture. Disciples of Jesus must give up everything to follow Jesus—they must give 100 percent. A disciple of Jesus is called to place total, unconditional trust in God the Father, as Jesus did.

The Rewards of Discipleship

Jesus told the wealthy young man the formula for discipleship: "Go, sell what you have, and give to [the] poor" (Mark 10:21). Mark reminds us that *everything* means *everything*. What a huge sacrifice—to give up everything! A great sacrifice does not go without a reward. The reward of being a disciple of Christ is eternal life—true wealth! Any sacrifice that is made now is surpassed by the future glory of heaven. The glory and happiness of heaven far exceed anything we can think of or comprehend in this life.

Mark concludes this Gospel story with a statement that summarizes a key point in Jesus' teaching:

"[M]any that are first will be last, and [the] last will be first."

MARK 10:31

People in Jesus' time saw persons of wealth as most often having the first place. Today we see persons of wealth, fame, and power as having seats on the fifty-yard line, vacationing in places most people can only dream about, or sending their children to the finest of colleges. Jesus asks us to take a second look at our lives. The measure for success here on earth that disciples of Jesus use is not the same measure that others use.

Heart in Hand. Larry Moore, contemporary painter.

FAITH CONNECTION

Think about a situation in your life when it cost you to be a disciple of Christ. Write and then say a prayer of thanksgiving to God for giving you the grace to make the decision to follow Jesus faithfully.

_____

_____

_____

Saint Martin de Porres

Each of us will have to make the decision as to what to do to live a successful life. The Church offers many models of people who have listened to the words of Jesus to "Go, sell what you have . . . then come, follow me" (Mark 10:21). Saint Martin de Porres (1579–1639) is one of those models.

After the Spanish explorer Pizarro (1471–1541) conquered Peru, Spain came to rule the Indians and blacks living in Peru. There were three very distinct groups of people in society: the Spanish, the Indians, and the blacks. And all of these groups despised anyone of mixed race. It was into this society that Martin de Porres was born in 1579 of a Spanish nobleman and a free black woman.

Martin learned a trade, that of a barber. In those times a barber was also a doctor, a surgeon, and a pharmacist. He became a success, being known as a healer and a hero to both blacks and Indians. But as fast as he made money, he gave it to the poor. By the time he was eighteen, Martin realized he wanted to dedicate his life to God.

Martin entered the Dominican monastery and was assigned to the infirmary to care for the sick. But not all people wanted to accept Martin's help since he had one white and one black parent. Martin understood that all his material goods were merely a means to an end. That end was to help others. His strong prayer life gave him the endurance needed to serve the poor throughout his sixty years of life.

In what ways can you put into practice the Gospel values modeled by Saint Martin de Porres?

Saint Martin de Porres. M. P. Wiggins, contemporary American artist/illustrator.

"Go, sell what you have ... then come, follow me."

Mark 10:21

WHAT DIFFERENCE
Does Faith Make in My Life?

What Is a Simple Life?

Saint Martin de Porres is one model of someone who responded to Jesus' call to be a disciple. Jesus also calls you to discipleship. As Jesus invited the wealthy man to "sell what you have . . . then come, follow me" (Mark 10:21), he is calling you to live a life free of clutter and unnecessary material possessions. This means instead of clinging to worldly things such as money, power, games, and expensive clothes, you are asked to be detached from these things. Jesus is not asking you to be homeless or to be totally without the things you need. He asks you to love and trust him for what you need and to share what you have with others. Jesus is asking you to live a simple life.

Time Is Money

There is a popular saying that "time is money." Living a simple life means that you are more concerned with having time to share with those you love and living as a disciple of Jesus in all you do. It means that money is used to acquire the things you really "need" rather than to squander it on possessions that you do not really need. For example: Can you feel free to buy a regular pair of shoes, rather than feel you absolutely must have the expensive designer shoes? Why would you buy the name-brand clothes? Is it because it is a status symbol to have expensive and popular things?

To live a simple life means to have an attitude of gratitude for what you have and a philosophy of life that you choose to follow. Jesus asks you to put your faith and trust in him and your God-given ability to do what you have to do to make things work out for the best. To be a true disciple of Jesus, your God, you are asked to follow him and not to follow the path that makes money, possessions, or fame your god.

What Can You Do?

Simplify your life; start now to free yourself of attachments to possessions.

Internalize your happiness; develop an attitude of gratitude as your goal.

Money can be used for needs, not just for more things you want.

Positively look at your choices; be free of society's pressures.

Live a life free of clutter and without tons of stuff.

Identify what is really important to you by looking inside yourself.

Freedom is to own your life and your choices so you can live a full, happy life.

You choose what is important to you, what you need to buy or own.

Limit your desire for more stuff; live freely and simply.

Involve yourself with family and friends, and things you like to do.

Faith in God, in life, and in people will lead you to trust that things will work out.

Enjoy your experiences, enjoy living simply, and use your energy for good.

Faith Decision

- Pick one thing on the "What Can You Do?" list that you are already doing. Share with a partner how you are doing it.

- Choose one thing from the list that you would like to *begin* doing to simplify your life.

This week I will choose to _____

_____.

I will begin to do it by _____

_____

_____.

PRAY and REVIEW

A Prayer of a Disciple of Jesus Christ

All: In the name of the Father,
and of the Son,
and of the Holy Spirit. Amen.

Leader: Father, you have sent us the
gift of the Holy Spirit
to teach and guide us to
live as disciples of your
Son, Jesus.
We gather in his name
to thank you.

All: Amen.

Reader: Proclaim John 15:13–14.

All: Silently reflect on the choices
they have made to live as
disciples of Christ and silently
give thanks for the gift of
being a disciple of Jesus.

Leader: Let us join together and pray
as Jesus taught us.

All: Our Father, who art in heaven,
hallowed be thy name;
thy kingdom come,
thy will be done on earth
as it is in heaven.
Give us this day our daily bread,
and forgive us our trespasses,
as we forgive those who
trespass against us;
and lead us not into temptation,
but deliver us from evil.
Amen.

*Share a sign of peace with
one another.*

FAITH VOCABULARY

Define the faith term *Evangelists*.

MAIN IDEAS

Choose either (a) or (b) from each set of items.
Write a brief paragraph to answer each of
your choices.
1. (a) What does Jesus tell the wealthy
young man he has to do to gain
eternal life?
   (b) Describe the wealthy young man's
response to Jesus.
2. (a) Describe what it means to be a
disciple of Jesus.
   (b) Explain the reward for faithfully
following Jesus.

CRITICAL THINKING

Using what you have learned in this chapter,
briefly explain this teaching of Jesus:
"Whoever wishes to come after me must
deny himself, take up his cross, and follow
me. For whoever wishes to save his life will
lose it, but whoever loses his life for my sake
and that of the gospel will save it. What
profit is there for one to gain the whole world
and forfeit his life? What could one give in
exchange for his life?" MARK 8:34–37

FAMILY DISCUSSION

In our family what do we work at the hardest?
Compare your answers to this question with Jesus'
answer to the wealthy young man's question.

For more ideas on ways
your family can live your
faith, visit the "Faith First
for Families" page at
www.FaithFirst.com. Also
click on the Teen Center and
check out "Bible Zone."

The Decision to Live Our Life in Christ

3

How is living a Christian moral life a path to freedom?

morality	natural law
sin	mortal sin
venial sin	conscience

Who are some of the people you have learned about who have made a positive contribution to building a just society?

Many people have been lights in our world during the last millennium. Their vision and works have made a vast difference in the course of human events. Blessed Pope John XXIII (1881–1963) and Blessed Mother Teresa of Calcutta (1910–1997) are two of these people. They both were humble people who believed that the path to a moral life was filled with simple daily choices to show love to others.

What are some simple choices that show you are living in Christ?

"[Y]our light must shine before others."
MATTHEW 5:16

Christian Morality: Living Our Life in Christ

Blessed Pope John XXIII and Blessed Mother Teresa of Calcutta took these words of Jesus seriously:

"[Y]our light must shine before others, that they may see your good deeds and glorify your heavenly Father." MATTHEW 5:16

The way we live our life in Christ is called the Christian moral life. **Morality** is the term that describes the way we have been created to live. In fact, the root word for *morality* is *morals*, a word that means "the way of life for a group of people."

Christian morality is the way of living for those who have been joined to Christ, the Light of the world, in Baptism. This way of life has been revealed to us by God and is based on:

- the life and teachings of Jesus Christ;
- the Scriptures;
- the working of the Holy Spirit in the Church, in the world, and in our lives; and
- the teachings of the Church.

Saint Paul the Apostle taught:

[Y]ou too must think of yourself as [being] dead to sin and living for God in Christ Jesus. . . . For sin is not to have any power over you, since you are not under the law but under grace. . . . What then? Shall we sin because we are not under the law but under grace? Of course not! . . . For the wages of sin is death, but the gift of God is eternal life in Christ Jesus our Lord. ROMANS 6:11, 14–15, 23

For the followers of Jesus, living a moral life is not simply about following a long list of laws. The Christian moral life is more about freely responding to God the Father, and the Son, and the Holy Spirit.

Do not misunderstand Saint Paul's teaching. Being "not under the law but under grace" does not mean we can do anything we like. Saint Paul was affirming how blessed we are: The Holy Spirit has been given to us. The Holy Spirit helps us know how to live as children of God and gives us the strength to choose freely to live our lives as Christ taught us.

Out of gratitude for the gift of our new life in Christ, we act with generosity and compassion toward others. We bring light into their lives as Christ, the Light of the world, taught us to do.

Define the term Christian morality in your own words.

Easter Proclamation during Service of the Light at the Easter Vigil

Certain factors can impact both our freedom to choose and the responsibility for our choices. Fear or pressure, as well as other psychological or social factors, can diminish or even erase our responsibility for any given action.

Through a life of prayer, reading the Scriptures, and learning the teachings of the Church, we strive to live as lights in our world. With the Holy Spirit's grace we strive to know and do what is good, and recognize and reject what is evil.

One of our inalienable rights as human beings is the right to exercise freedom, especially in religious and moral matters. Without this freedom we would not be able to give ourselves to God and freely accept God's gift of himself to us.

Did you Know...

The Old Testament Book of Proverbs is a book of short sayings that give practical advice on how to make sound moral choices. The writers used many literary techniques to make the sayings memorable.

Confused by Road Signs. Eric Westbrook, contemporary American illustrator.

The Gift of Freedom of Choice

Free will and intellect, or reason, make us responsible for our own actions. They give us the power to know and choose between what is good and what is evil. They give us the power to bring either light or darkness to the world. The Scriptures remind us:

> If you choose you can keep the commandments;
> it is loyalty to do his will.
> SIRACH 15:15

FAITH CONNECTION

Create a sign that directs us to follow the way of Christ.

Making Moral Decisions

Living our life in Christ is a 24/7, lifelong calling. Living our life in Christ takes place right here, right now. We need to deal with the moral issues that meet us face-to-face each day. How do we know that we are on the right track?

The Natural Law

God has placed within us a **natural law.** The natural law is the foundation of the moral life of everyone—Christians and non-Christians. It is the original sense of right and wrong that is part of every human being. It enables us by human reason to know good and evil. It guides us to discover the way to true happiness that God has created everyone to have. It helps us recognize the evil that leads us away from that happiness and away from God.

Elements of Moral Actions

The moral life we live is formed by the choices we make. The goodness or evil of our actions depends on three things. These are:

- **What we choose to do.** This is called the *object* of our moral act. It is what we knowingly choose to do or not to do. Some objects, such as adultery and murder, trashing another person's reputation, and theft, are always wrong.

- **Why we choose.** This is called the *intention* of our moral act. Our intention, or motive, for choosing a moral act affects the goodness or evil of an act. A good intention can never turn an evil act into a good act.

A bad intention, however, can turn a good act into an evil one. For example, you go out of your way to compliment your teacher. You do this only because you want to use this teacher to write a letter of recommendation for you. The compliment is a good act; the letter is a good end. Your motive, your intention, is tainted. So is the act.

- **The details surrounding the act.** We call these the *circumstances* of a moral act. The circumstances include the *how, who, when,* and *where* of the act. Such circumstances can increase or lessen the goodness or evil of a moral act.

Explain the three elements of moral actions.

Turning Away from God's Love

In the face of all we have been taught and all the bells and whistles going off inside our heads warning us not to do something, we nevertheless sometimes freely ignore them. We sometimes freely and knowingly do what is against God's law. When we do, we **sin**. When we deliberately lead others to sin gravely, we commit the sin of scandal. Sin sets us against God and turns our hearts away from his love.

Mortal Sin

When we commit some sins, we choose to turn our backs totally on God. The Church uses the term **mortal sin** to describe these sins. The word *mortal* means "deadly." A mortal sin causes the loss of sanctifying grace. It kills completely the life of grace within us.

Unrepented mortal sin brings eternal death. We can, of course, find forgiveness of mortal sins and restore our life with God through the proper celebration of the sacrament of Reconciliation.

Venial Sin

Venial sin involves a less serious offense against God. It does not cause the loss of sanctifying grace. Sins are venial when (1) we do not do something that is in itself gravely, or seriously, evil; or (2) we do not have *full* knowledge of the act's sinfulness; or (3) we do not have complete freedom in making our choice. We should not take venial sins lightly. The idea that they are less serious does not mean that it really does not matter that we commit them.

All sin turns our hearts away from God's love. Getting into the habit of committing venial sins can set us up to sin more seriously.

Work with a group. Discuss a situation in which small, habitual sins can eventually lead to a more serious sin.

Did you Know...

The pope and the bishops are our allies in forming our conscience. When they speak, we do well to listen. They are guided by the Holy Spirit to teach us without error the true meaning of what God has revealed about the Ten Commandments, the Beatitudes, and other moral teachings about loving God, others, and ourselves.

The Gift of Conscience

Christian life is made up of choices. Within us there is a persistent voice that helps us make these choices. We call this voice our **conscience.**

Every human being has a conscience. It helps us judge right from wrong. A well-formed conscience helps us see things more clearly. Whether we are about to do something or are in the middle of doing it or even have finished the act, our conscience is at work.

When we honestly work at building a well-formed conscience and follow it, we are building a guide that, with the Holy Spirit's help, will lead us toward God and eternal happiness.

Fork in the Road. Richard Mandrachio, contemporary American illustrator.

If we choose not to follow a well-formed conscience, we will choose a path away from God. When we do, our conscience will make itself heard. It will call us to take responsibility for our actions. Our conscience will confront us with the truth and invite us to make a better choice. It will call us to repair any damage we may have caused and return to the path that truly leads to happiness.

Word in Your Ear. Illustrator unknown.

FAITH CONNECTION

Create a cartoonlike illustration in which "Conscience" is a character who is helping a friend make a decision.

Retreats and Retreat Houses

Jesus taught that his disciples are to let their light shine before others so that others may see their good deeds and glorify their heavenly Father (see Matthew 5:16). Making, or going on, a retreat is one way Christians work at doing what Jesus taught. When we make a retreat, we spend time in prayerful reflection evaluating the way we are faithfully following Jesus' command to be lights in the world.

The Church funds, sponsors, and staffs many retreat houses throughout the country. There are camping retreats, silent retreats, corporate retreats, family retreats, teen retreats, music retreats, confirmation retreats, and many other types of retreats. One quality that all retreats have in common is they get us to break away from the normal routine and take time to think and pray. We step away and examine ourselves, our habits, our past decisions and choices, and, most importantly, our relationship with God.

Retreats give us an opportunity to reflect on our lives and compare what we discover about ourselves with who God wants us to be. They empower us to reenter our daily lives with a renewed relationship with God and with others.

What are some ways that would help you reflect on the way you are living your life in Christ now?

WHAT DIFFERENCE

Does Faith Make in My Life?

Informed Conscience

Our conscience is a gift from God that helps us make the right decisions to live our lives as God created us to do. Our conscience guides us in our Christian attitude, our actions, and our choices.

You are constantly making decisions that not only have an effect on you but also have a positive or negative effect on other people. To help you make the right moral decisions, you need to develop a well-formed conscience. This is very important since we have the responsibility to obey our conscience.

It is not always easy to make the right choice, but a well-formed conscience and the grace of the Holy Spirit will help you do so. Usually, you make a certain choice because you believe it will make you happy. A well-formed conscience can help you examine whether that choice is a responsible Christian decision or if that choice will harm you or other people. Here are some steps to take to help you develop a well-formed moral conscience.

- **Always think before you act.** Imagine Jesus standing right there with you.
- **Remember the choices Jesus made.** You have heard about and read about the choices Jesus made in the Gospels. Read some of these Gospel stories again.
- **Remember the teachings of the Catholic Church.** The Church is our Mother and Teacher. She teaches us how to be a faithful follower of Jesus.

Man in Question Mark Maze. Paul Schulenburg, contemporary American illustrator.

- **Pray to the Holy Spirit.** Open your mind and heart to the grace of the Holy Spirit to guide you in making wise and responsible choices.
- **Receive the sacraments.** Take part in the celebrations of Reconciliation and Eucharist often and regularly.

When you make good Christian decisions, you take responsibility for your choices. If you are choosing to avoid sin, you are choosing right from wrong and looking at the consequences of your actions. Sometimes a choice will have a far-reaching effect or even change your life forever.

Remember that you have no control over the choices of others, but sometimes you may feel the results of their choices. It can be very helpful to talk with your family, your religious leaders, and your friends about some of the concerns you have about making the right decisions. Choose some positive role models who have shown by their example that they have an informed moral conscience and that they can make the right choices.

Faith · Decision

- Role-play a typical situation in which someone is trying to make a responsible choice to live as a follower of Christ.

- Tell how your example illustrates at least one of the steps on pages 36 and 37.

This week choose one of the steps described on pages 36 and 37 to help you continue to develop a well-formed conscience. Write what you will do here:

_____

_____

_____

PRAY and REVIEW

Prayer for Guidance

The Psalms express the desire of the People of God to live as the People of God. Psalm 139 expresses the faith in the ever-present God, who always knows and guides his people.

All: **Lord, you see me and you know me.**

Group 1: You know when I sit. You know when I stand. You know what I think.

All: **Lord, you see me and you know me.**

Group 2: You know where I go. You know when I sleep. You know everything I do.

All: **Lord, you see me and you know me.**

Group 1: Before I speak, you know what I will say.

All: **Lord, you see me and you know me.**

Group 2: You are in front of me. You are behind me. You are all around me.

All: **Tell me if my way is wrong, and lead me on the path you have taught me.**

BASED ON PSALM 139:1–7, 24

FAITH VOCABULARY

Define each of these faith vocabulary terms:

1. morality
2. natural law
3. sin
4. mortal sin
5. venial sin
6. conscience

MAIN IDEAS

Choose either (a) or (b) from each set of items. Write a brief paragraph to answer each of your choices.

1. (a) Name the four elements on which Christian morality is based.
   (b) Describe the sources of morality.

2. (a) Describe the steps in developing a well-formed conscience.
   (b) Explain the meaning of the adage "Let your conscience be your guide."

CRITICAL THINKING

Using what you have learned in this chapter, briefly explain this statement:
"[Conscience] is a messenger of him . . . who . . . speaks to us from behind a veil."
JOHN HENRY CARDINAL NEWMAN (1801–1890)

FAMILY DISCUSSION

Discuss this statement as a family: It is just as important for us to be lights to one another in our family as it is for us to be lights to others in the world outside our home.

For more ideas on ways your family can live your faith, visit the "Faith First for Families" page at **www.FaithFirst.com**. Also check out the Teen Center and read this week's interactive story.

Hymn of Love

A Scripture Story

4

FAITH FOCUS

What is the message of the First Letter to the Corinthians?

FAITH VOCABULARY

evangelize   love

What are some situations in your life that can lead to disagreements and arguments?

Imagine that a well-liked teacher has started a club at your school. After spending several years working with students in building the club, the teacher is transferred to another school. Soon, disagreements arise over the purpose and programs of the club. The members begin taking sides—one group against another. The club seems to be falling apart. The early Church experienced similar difficult times and divisions. When these divisions were resolved, there was a much deeper harmony within the Church.

What kinds of things might the first Christians have argued about?

Love never fails.
1 CORINTHIANS 13:8

The Church at Corinth

Corinth was a seaport city-state in ancient Greece surrounded by mountains and farmlands. Located midway between Sparta and Athens, it served as a center of trade around the Mediterranean Sea during the life of Saint Paul the Apostle. During his second missionary journey in A.D. 51, Saint Paul **evangelized**, or proclaimed the Gospel, in Corinth. The people who asked for Baptism included a mixture of Jews and Greeks and other ethnic groups. Many of those people were from the middle and lower classes. Most were Gentiles, or non-Jews.

Saint Paul stayed at Corinth for approximately a year and a half. He established a Christian community there and supported his missionary efforts by working as a tentmaker.

After his stay in Corinth, Paul traveled throughout the Mediterranean. When he was in Ephesus, in today's Turkey, Paul learned about divisions within the Church in Corinth. He responded by writing a letter. In the letter Paul answered some of the questions the believers in Corinth had asked him. He also sought to correct some of the abuses that had arisen in the Church in Corinth after he had departed.

Factions

Forgetting that Christ was the source of their unity, members of the Church in Corinth were splitting into factions. They were grouping together around the person who initially proclaimed the Gospel to them—Paul or Apollos or Cephas. In strong terms, Saint Paul tried to put an end to these divisions by making it clear that no Christian belonged to Paul or Apollos or Cephas. All belonged to Christ.

Explain Saint Paul's teaching about the unity of the Church.

Ruins of the ancient city of Acrocorinth

The Worshiping Community

Saint Paul also addressed a number of issues that were dividing the worshiping assembly. Among these issues were the conduct of the Corinthians at the celebration of the Lord's Supper (see 1 Corinthians 11:17–34) and the importance of the spiritual gifts given to the Church (see 1 Corinthians 12:1–11). The use of these gifts was dividing the community more and more because the Corinthians had lost sight of the very reason the Holy Spirit had given these gifts to the Church—for the good of the Body of Christ.

As the Church in Corinth began to grow, other questions about Saint Paul's teachings about Jesus and how to live the way of Jesus began to arise. Not all the answers the Corinthians came up with on their own were correct. Deeply distressed, Saint Paul wrote the First Letter to the Corinthians to put them back on the right track:

> I urge you, brothers, in the name of our Lord Jesus Christ, that all of you agree in what you say, and that there be no divisions among you, but that you be united in the same mind and in the same purpose.
>
> 1 CORINTHIANS 1:10

Saint Paul, Apostle to the Gentiles, stained glass

Did you Know...

The New Testament contains thirteen Pauline letters. Most Scripture scholars agree that Paul definitely wrote seven of these. They are Romans, First Corinthians, Second Corinthians, Galatians, Philippians, First Thessalonians, and Philemon. While the other six letters contain the teachings of the Apostle, they were probably written by Paul's disciples. These letters are Ephesians, Colossians, Second Thessalonians, First Timothy, Second Timothy, and Titus.

FAITH CONNECTION

With a group, create a saying that can remind Christians to put aside differences and remember what is most important.

_____

_____

_____

_____

_____

_____

_____

Cross, symbol for faith; anchor, symbol for hope; heart, symbol for love

A Hymn of Love

While the members of the Body of Christ, the Church, have different functions and responsibilities, each and every member is important. Each and every member has been gifted in some way by the Holy Spirit to build up the Church on earth and to live out their life in Christ. Saint Paul reminded the Corinthians that each member's gifts, if they are used without **love**, are useless:

> If I speak in human and angelic tongues but do not have love, I am a resounding gong or a clashing cymbal. And if I have the gift of prophecy and comprehend all mysteries and all knowledge; if I have all faith so as to move mountains but do not have love, I am nothing. If I give away everything I own, and if I hand my body over so that I may boast but do not have love, I gain nothing.
>
> 1 CORINTHIANS 13:1–3

Saint Paul then describes the qualities of love. He continues:

> Love is patient, love is kind. It is not jealous, [love] is not pompous, it is not inflated, it is not rude, it does not seek its own interests, it is not quick-tempered, it does not brood over injury, it does not rejoice over wrongdoing but rejoices with the truth. It bears all things, believes all things, hopes all things, endures all things.
>
> 1 CORINTHIANS 13:4–7

What is the relationship between the theological virtue of love and the virtues of faith and hope?

Saint Paul concludes by emphasizing that living a life of love is at the heart of living as a disciple of Christ. He continues:

Love never fails. If there are prophecies, they will be brought to nothing; if tongues, they will cease; if knowledge, it will be brought to nothing. For we know partially and we prophesy partially, but when the perfect comes, the partial will pass away. When I was a child, I used to talk as a child, think as a child, reason as a child; when I became a man, I put aside childish things. At present we see indistinctly, as in a mirror, but then face to face. At present I know partially; then I shall know fully, as I am fully known. So faith, hope, love remain, these three; but the greatest of these is love.

1 CORINTHIANS 13:8–13

The greatest of all the gifts of the Holy Spirit is love. Love is the only gift that is permanent and is superior to all other gifts. Love is the gift that unifies the Church, the Body of Christ. Love is the one gift which is the foundation of the way the Church must live.

Why does Saint Paul say that love is the greatest of gifts?

Faith Hope Love the greatest of these is Love

Practical Advice

Saint Paul's teaching on love as the more excellent way is a practical and potent piece of spiritual wisdom. Is there any doubt that Paul would focus on love to heal the divisions within the Church at Corinth? Saint Paul chose his words very carefully to emphasize that the lack of love was the reason other virtues were not being lived. For example, he pointed out that:

- those who were strong were not being patient and kind (see 1 Corinthians 13:4).
- too often there was rejoicing "over wrongdoing" (see 1 Corinthians 13:6).
- those who took false pride in their superior wisdom (see 1 Corinthians 1:18–2:16) needed to consider how partial and halting knowledge is (see 1 Corinthians 13:12).
- those who felt their particular gifts were superior to the gifts of others needed to realize that the greatest gift of all is love (see 1 Corinthians 13:13).

The bottom line is that Saint Paul was admonishing the Corinthians that it was time to change their ways and base their lives on Jesus' command:

"I give you a new commandment: love one another. As I have loved you, so you also should love one another. This is how all will know that you are my disciples, if you have love for one another."

JOHN 13:34–35

Take Another Look!

Today, as the world grows closer through communications and travel, we are experiencing an ever-widening division among peoples. The dignity that unites all people as children of God is often ignored and even blatantly cast aside. The evils of racism and bigotry and prejudice seem to flourish as if they were social virtues. Barriers of social class and wealth are built higher and higher and are oppressing the poor more and more. Violence on streets and in schools and in neighborhoods speaks more of hatred than of love.

FAITH CONNECTION

Compare two current news events, one event showing people living Saint Paul's teaching on love and the other event showing people not living Paul's teaching. Share your comparisons with a partner.

Living Paul's Teaching	Not Living Paul's Teaching

OUR CHURCH
MAKES A DIFFERENCE

L'Arche Communities

Jean Vanier and the members of L'Arche communities live the ideals named in Paul's hymn of love in a unique way. Jean Vanier started a home in a small village in France for people with developmental disabilities. Jean called the home L'Arche, a French word meaning "the Ark" or "the Covenant." It is a symbol of love and hope and of the Covenant that God has made with all people.

L'Arche community is truly a way of life, not a program. At L'Arche everyone is appreciated for who they are as a person. It makes no difference what you have or what you can do. Members put into practice Paul's hymn of love. Jean Vanier describes love this way:

> Love has a transforming power. It is first and foremost a revelation of a person's essential, fundamental beauty and value. If nobody reveals to children their innate beauty and value, they will never know the importance and meaning of their life.

L'Arche community is a way to live out the Gospel today. Since the first L'Arche community began in 1964, the number of L'Arche communities has grown to more than one hundred in thirty countries throughout the world.

What can you learn from the vision of Jean Vanier? How can you put that vision into practice?

Jean Vanier (right) with
L'Arche community members

L'Arche community,
Spokane, Washington state

WHAT DIFFERENCE
Does Faith Make in My Life?

Love Really Is . . .

Think about the number of songs, poems, movies, stories, DVDs, TV shows, works of art, cards, magazines, and Internet sites that explore the topic of love. Yet with all this attention given to love, there is still great confusion over the true meaning of love.

More than two thousand years ago, Paul attempted to explain to the Corinthians what love is and what it is not. While these inspired words of the Bible have been read at marriage ceremonies countless times, this famous description of Christian love is not only for married couples. It gives us all a formula for living our relationships in the way God—who is love—is always calling us to live.

Each of your relationships is unique and different in some ways from the others. But God is calling you to love all people, and Paul's definition of love can be applied to all relationships.

Relationships

Think of a relationship that is important in your life right now. As you read each part of Saint Paul's teaching on love, substitute your name for the word *love*. Then explain how you put this teaching into practice.

Love (_____) is patient when

_____
_____ .

Love (_____) is kind when

_____
_____ .

Love (_____) is not jealous when _____

_____ .

Love (_____) is not quick-tempered when _____

_____ .

Love (_____) is not rude when _____

_____ .

Love (_____) does not rejoice over wrongdoings when

_____
_____ .

Love (_____) is not pompous when _____

_____ .

Love (_____) is not selfish when _____

_____ .

If each of us could really love this way, as we are all called to do, we would truly have the ingredients for healthy, happy, and life-giving relationships.

Faith Decision

- Have a discussion with a parent, a brother, a sister, or a friend about Saint Paul's teachings on love. Choose one characteristic of love named by Saint Paul you will both agree to work on to make your relationship stronger.

- Take time this week to think about and evaluate your relationships with God, with self, and with others. Decide what you can do to strengthen them and make them healthy.

This week I will choose one of the expressions of love described by Saint Paul and put it into practice by

_____
_____
_____
_____
_____ .

PRAY and REVIEW

Love Never Ends

A prayer of petition asks God to help us live as he commands us to do. In a prayer of petition, we ask God for the grace to change our hearts and live the virtue of love that keeps God at the center of our lives.

Leader: Saint Paul teaches: "Love bears all things, believes all things, hopes all things, endures all things" (BASED ON 1 CORINTHIANS 13:4–7). Let us pray, asking God's help to live in Christ's love.

Reader 1: For all the times we are impatient and unkind,

All: **change our hearts, O Lord.**

Reader 2: For all the times we are jealous, arrogant, or rude,

All: **change our hearts, O Lord.**

Reader 3: For all the times we are selfish, irritable, or ill-tempered,

All: **change our hearts, O Lord.**

Reader 4: For all the times we do not tell the truth,

All: **change our hearts, O Lord.**

Reader 5: For all the times we seek our own interests and neglect the needs of others,

All: **change our hearts, O Lord. Amen.**

FAITH VOCABULARY

Use the faith terms *evangelize* and *love* correctly in a sentence.

MAIN IDEAS

Choose either (a) or (b) from each set of items. Write a brief paragraph to answer each of your choices.

1. (a) Why was the First Letter to the Corinthians written?
   (b) Describe the qualities of love that Paul names in the First Letter to the Corinthians.

2. (a) Describe the teaching of Jesus on which Paul bases his hymn of love in the First Letter to the Corinthians.
   (b) What situations in our world can we reexamine in light of Paul's teaching on love?

CRITICAL THINKING

Using what you have learned in this chapter, briefly explain this Scripture verse:
[I]f I have all faith so as to move mountains, but do not have love, I am nothing.

1 CORINTHIANS 13:2

FAMILY DISCUSSION

What are some things we can do as a family to put into practice the gift of love as described by Saint Paul?

For more ideas on ways your family can live your faith, visit the "Faith First for Families" page at **www.FaithFirst.com**. Also check out the extra activity for this chapter on the Teen Center.

The Exercise of Virtue

5

FAITH FOCUS

How does the practice of the virtues help us grow in living the Great Commandment?

FAITH VOCABULARY

virtues   theological virtues

moral virtues   society

common good   social sin

When have you practiced doing little things better so you could achieve a bigger goal?

Did you ever wonder how history's heroes became heroes? Practice! Practice is also the method by which great saints progress in their vocations of being other-Christs. Unlike thugs, however, saints practice virtues rather than vices.

FROM *JESUS BEYOND 2000* BY MARK LINK

What are some of the virtues the saints practiced?

[T]he fruit of noble struggles is a glorious one.
WISDOM 3:15

Staying on the Right Course

Living the Virtues

Christian living is about practice too. It is about living the **virtues.** Virtues build healthy relationships both with God and with other people. Virtues are spiritual powers or habits or behaviors. They help us do what is right and avoid what is wrong. They are firm dispositions, or attitudes. They strengthen us to live the new life in Christ that we receive in Baptism.

The Theological Virtues

Christian tradition speaks of theological virtues and moral virtues. The **theological virtues** are faith, hope, and charity. The word *theological* means "belonging to God." Theological virtues are the strengths or habits that God gives us to help us attain holiness. They link us more closely with God the Father, Son, and Holy Spirit. They are the pillars on which our life in Christ is built.

Faith. Faith is the gift of God's invitation to believe in him. It is also the ability and power God gives us to respond to his invitation.

Hope. Hope is the virtue that helps us keep our eyes on the kingdom of heaven. It enables us to trust in God and in his promises above all else.

Charity. Charity is the virtue that enables us to love God simply because he is God. It also enables us to love our neighbor as ourselves because of our love for God. Love is the greatest of all the virtues (see 1 Corinthians 13:13). It gives life and form to all the other virtues.

Describe the three theological virtues. Describe how living the virtues helps us obtain holiness.

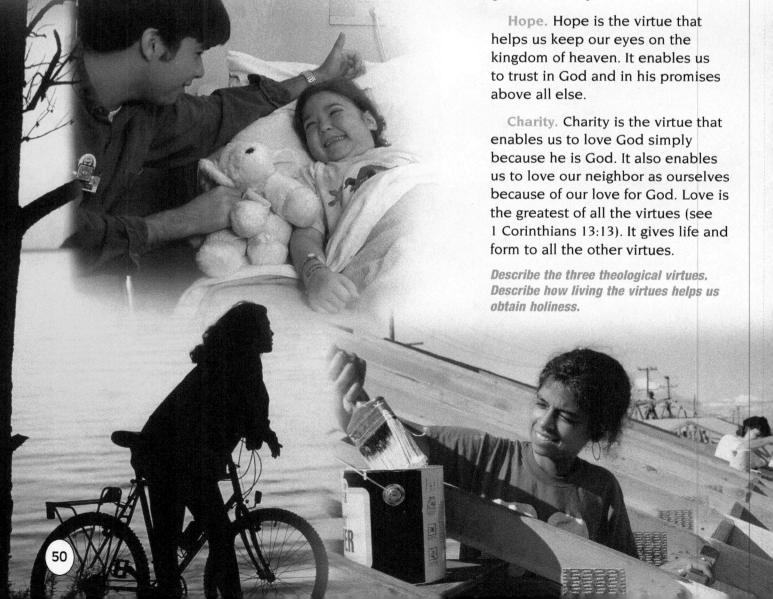

The Moral Virtues

Prudence, justice, fortitude, and temperance are the four **moral**, or cardinal, **virtues**. The word *cardinal* comes from a Latin word meaning "hinge." Our moral life and our moral decision making hinge on the development and practice of the four cardinal virtues.

The more we cooperate with the Holy Spirit, the more we develop these virtues. The more we develop the moral virtues, the better able we will be to make decisions to live as children of God and followers of Christ.

Did you Know...

The signs that show a person is living the virtues are called the fruits of the Holy Spirit. They are love, joy, peace, patience, kindness, generosity, gentleness, faithfulness, and self-control (see Galatians 5:19–26).

FAITH CONNECTION

Choose one of the theological virtues. List times when the practice of this virtue would be needed.

_____

_____

_____

_____

Social Creatures

Virtues give expression to our finest human values: love of God and neighbor, honesty, integrity, responsibility, and so on. Living the virtues includes making deliberate and knowledgeable decisions. The virtues also guide us in using our emotions, or feelings, to live as children of God and followers of Christ.

God created us in his image and likeness. He created us to live together in a way that resembles the Holy Trinity, in whose image we have been created. He has created us as social creatures that are to live in community.

Society is a special form of community. A society is "a group of people distinct from other groups and sharing a common culture, common interests, and common activities." A society is made up of many types of smaller communities—families, schools, workplaces, and towns, cities, and nations.

The Common Good

Striving to live the Great Commandment (see Matthew 22:36–39) in the communities we belong to, both as individuals and as a society, is what life is all about. Achieving this goal is the **common good** of all the members of society.

Background: *Save the World.*
Diane Ong (1946–),
Chinese-American painter.

Civic, or Social, Authority

Public authority has the responsibility and obligation to help individuals and the smaller communities work together for the common good. All authority flows from God. True authority in society supports all the members of society to live their lives according to God's plan of creation. Authority that leads its members away from living according to God's plan is a sham, a lie.

True civic authority maintains good order. It works for the true common good of the people. True authority creates the conditions for its members to achieve this common good by creating and enforcing just, moral, and equitable laws.

True authority inspires individuals to respect others. It serves the basic human needs for life, liberty, and the pursuit of happiness. True authority protects the freedom of its members to pursue living the Great Commandment according to their conscience. It creates the conditions that enable people to live the virtues and build their lives on true human values.

Give examples of proper and improper use of public authority.

Did you Know...

The Church has named several ways that members of society can show their respect for and support of one another. Based on the teachings of Jesus, these are called the Corporal Works of Mercy and the Spiritual Works of Mercy.

A Just Society

A society that truly works at achieving the common good is a just society. The word *just* is defined in many ways. These meanings include (1) honorable and fair, (2) morally right, righteous, (3) properly due or deserved, (4) based on good reason, well-founded, and (5) lawful.

A just society is first and foremost a morally right society. It is a society that guides and supports its members to live in a right relationship with God and others. The Church's teachings on social justice guide us in building a just society. (A summary of these teachings is found on page 143.)

Social Sin

Every society has the responsibility to create the conditions that enable people to live together in peace and justice. When public authority and citizens work together for the common good—when they keep in mind the well-being of one another—everyone gains. When individuals cooperate with one another and work against human life and human rights, they sin. We call this sin **social sin.** We take part in social sin when:

- we participate directly and freely in another person's sin.
- we order, advise, praise, or approve of another person's wrongdoing.
- we fail to appropriately disclose or hinder another person's sin when we have an opportunity to do so.
- we protect those who do evil.

Christians look to the Gospel for their inspiration and vision and the principles for building a just society. When we work together to build a just society according to the teachings of Jesus, we are preparing the way for the coming of the kingdom of God.

FAITH CONNECTION

What are some of the things you see people doing to build a just society?

_____

_____

_____

Peter Maurin

practice the Church's teachings on social justice and worked toward building a just society. In 1933 Dorothy Day and Peter Maurin founded the Catholic Worker movement. The original vision of the Catholic Worker community coincided with the havoc and suffering caused by the Great Depression (1929–1941). Dorothy Day set out to work with the victims of the Great Depression by establishing hospitality houses to provide food and shelter to those in need. Today there are more than 140 Catholic Worker communities committed to promoting the cause of justice and mercy among the poor and homeless. Dorothy Day and Peter Maurin not only served the poor but also voluntarily embraced living a life of poverty and simplicity.

The Catholic Worker is the name of the newspaper published by the Catholic Worker community. Dorothy Day was the editor of the newspaper during its first forty-seven years of publication. The price of the newspaper is still a penny a copy.

What are some of the ways you treat other people fairly?

Dorothy Day serving soup in Catholic Worker house

Catholic Worker Movement

Christian living is about building healthy relationships both with God and with other people. Another way of saying this is that Christian living is about building a just society. Dorothy Day (1897–1980) and Peter Maurin (1877–1949) put into

WHAT DIFFERENCE
Does Faith Make in My Life?

Moral Virtues in Our Lives

Practice makes perfect. When you intentionally practice a good habit or a positive attitude, it becomes easier for you to do. When you practice making good choices and living a good life, you are creating a habit. Moral virtues are good habits that help you make good choices and live a good moral life. Developing the four moral virtues of prudence, justice, fortitude, and temperance in your daily life can help you be a happier and better Christian.

Prudence

Prudence is practical wisdom that helps you choose what is good and choose the things necessary to do what is right. You are prudent if you:

❖ set aside time to do your homework first instead of putting it off until late in the night.

❖ look for new friends who share your values or beliefs if the friends you have are always getting into trouble.

❖ seek the help or advice of a wise and trusted adult when you find yourself in a difficult situation.

Justice

Justice gives you the strength to respect the rights of every person to receive a fair share of the blessings and goodness God has given to the world. You can practice justice by:

❖ always playing fair in games or in sports.

❖ treating people with respect.

❖ not being prejudiced because of color, beliefs, or social class.

❖ doing your best work in school and at home.

❖ not putting people down or making fun of them.

Fortitude

Fortitude is the strength and courage to do what is right and good. It enables you to:

❖ stand up for your values.

❖ overcome obstacles and try again.

❖ give whatever you are doing your best effort.

Temperance

Temperance is the attitude and habit that helps you exercise self-control. It helps you:

❖ maintain balance and moderation in everything you do.

❖ not be excessive or go overboard in whatever you are doing, even if no one is looking.

As you practice these good habits or virtues, you will also develop skills to live a good moral life. These virtues help you live and grow in your relationship with God and others.

Faith·
Decision

- Work with a partner or in a small group. Choose a movie, TV show, or book in which the characters display one or several of the moral virtues. Describe how the virtue or virtues affect the relationships between characters.

- Role-play for the whole class the situation you described.

This week I will practice the moral virtue of

_____.

I will _____

_____

_____

_____

_____.

PRAY and REVIEW

Prayer for the Easter Virtues

Place yourself in the presence of the Lord. Close your eyes and meditate on the events of the last days of his life on earth, one at a time. Open your eyes and quietly pray this prayer in your heart.

Lord Jesus,

your Resurrection
has given me
new life and
renewed hope.

Grant me
the wisdom
to know what I must do,

the will
to want to do it,

the courage
to undertake it,

the perseverance
to continue to do it,

and the strength
to complete it.

Amen.

FAITH VOCABULARY

Define each of these faith terms:

1. virtues
2. theological virtues
3. moral virtues
4. society
5. common good
6. social sin

MAIN IDEAS

Choose either (a) or (b) from each set of items. Write a brief paragraph to answer each of your choices.

1. (a) Describe the theological virtues of faith, hope, and charity.
   (b) Explain the importance of developing the moral virtues.
2. (a) Explain the common good of society.
   (b) Describe a just society.

CRITICAL THINKING

Using what you have learned in this chapter, briefly explain this Scripture verse:
"Much will be required of the person entrusted with much."   LUKE 12:48

FAMILY DISCUSSION

How can we as a family work to create a just society and prepare the way for the coming of the kingdom of God?

For more ideas on ways your family can live your faith, visit the "Faith First for Families" page at **www.FaithFirst.com**. Also remember to read the next chapter of the interactive story on the Teen Center.

The Grace of the Holy Spirit

6

Descent of Holy Spirit, stained glass

FAITH FOCUS

How does God share divine life and love with us?

FAITH VOCABULARY

grace

justification

merit

sanctifying grace

sanctification

What talents have you been given? How have you used or not used them?

A woman sees a sign in the window of a new gift shop at the mall. The sign reads, "No cost! No charge! All items free!" Without hesitation she enters and, much to her surprise, finds God tending the store. "What are you selling here?" the woman asks, somewhat hesitantly. "Nothing! Everything your soul desires is yours for the asking," responds God. Hardly believing her ears, the woman bravely decides upon her list. "I want peace on earth not just for myself, but for everyone on the planet." God smiles at her and responds, "You're on the right track, my child, but at this shop we don't stock fruits (as in results), only seeds."

What do you think is the meaning of this modern-day parable?

Grace to you and peace from God our Father and the Lord Jesus Christ.

PHILEMON 1:3

The New Life of Grace

Free and Undeserved Gift

Grace is like seed that God freely plants within us. The parable of the Sower (see Mark 4:1–20) helps us understand the role of grace in our lives.

A very large crowd gathered around [Jesus] so that he got into a boat on the sea and sat down. And the whole crowd was beside the sea on the land. And he taught them at length in parables, and in the course of his instruction he said to them, "Hear this! A sower went out to sow. And as he sowed, some seed fell on the path, and the birds came and ate it up. Other seed fell on rocky ground where it had little soil. It sprang up at once because the soil was not deep. And when the sun rose, it was scorched and it withered for lack of roots. Some seed fell among thorns, and the thorns grew up and choked it and it produced no grain. And some seed fell on rich soil and produced fruit. It came up and grew and yielded thirty, sixty, and a hundredfold." MARK 4:3–8

Then when he was alone with his disciples Jesus helped them understand the meaning of the parable. He explained that the seed that fell on the path and rocky ground and among the thorns either died or did not bear much fruit. He then explained:

"But those sown on rich soil are the ones who hear the word and accept it and bear fruit thirty and sixty and a hundredfold." MARK 4:20

We do not deserve this rich planting. God, the Sower, plants the seeds of faith, hope, and love in our hearts because of his love for us. God prepares the soil, plants the seeds, and provides the proper nutrients to ensure a bountiful crop.

Parable of the Sower,
stained glass

People Nursing Plant with Children. Ryoicho Yotsumoto, contemporary illustrator.

Grace is our participation in the very life of God, a sharing in the intimacy enjoyed by the Father, Son, and Holy Spirit. This grace is the free and undeserved gift by which we are united with God and which empowers us to love him who first loved us.

When unimpeded by our sin and when nurtured by faith, prayer, and the sacraments, grace will produce life in abundance for us. We will share in divine life "thirty, sixty, and a hundredfold" (Mark 4:8). These seeds of grace sown by God in our lives have the potential to yield a spectacular harvest.

God's love for us is so great that without taking away our freedom he responds to this deepest desire of our hearts. God not only places this desire within us but also strengthens us so that our search for that happiness can be successful.

While that is all true, it does not mean that all we do is sit back and let God tend the seeds he has planted within us. If that is our attitude, God's grace and his word will not bear much fruit in our lives. The life of grace within us can wither or be choked up and produce nothing.

The Latin word *gratia* is the source of many English words. *Gratia* means "thanks," "charm," or "favor." From the Latin word *gratia* we also get words like *gratitude*, *gracious*, *gratuity*, and, of course, *grace*. Remember the words of the angel to Mary: "Do not be afraid, Mary, for you have found favor with God" (Luke 1:30). The Hail Mary states this greeting this way: "Hail Mary, full of grace."

FAITH CONNECTION

Work with a group. Brainstorm a situation challenging Catholic youth to live their faith. Apply the parable of the Sower to the situation and describe how they might act if they were the

"path" _____

_____

"rocky ground" _____

_____

"soil among thorns" _____

_____

"rich soil" _____

_____

Baptism, stained glass, symbolizing freedom from sin (left) and gift of the Holy Spirit (right)

the Holy Spirit at Baptism, sanctifying grace is the love of God entering our souls, healing us from sin, and restoring our holiness. It is our sharing in the life of God the Father, Son, and Holy Spirit.

Justification

Through Baptism we receive new life in Christ and the gift of the Holy Spirit. New life in Christ is a gift God totally gives on his own. It is not something we could ever earn on our own. This gift of new life in Christ is described by the word **justification**, which means "the process of making one just." In Christ and through his Paschal Mystery, humanity and, indeed, all of creation are once again made just. We are set in right relationship with God. What our first parents lost for themselves and all creatures, original justice, Jesus restored.

Through faith in Jesus and the cleansing power of Baptism, we are justified. In other words, in and through and with Christ alone, we are justified. Jesus, who is both God and man, truly human and truly divine, repairs our lost friendship with God. He sets us in right order with God again.

Explain the meaning of the term justification in your own words.

The New Law of Grace

Grace makes us alive in Christ and Christ alive in us (see Romans 6:8–11). Before Christ's life, death, and Resurrection, humanity was under the power of sin and death. In Christ, the new Adam, all that changed. By the Paschal Mystery of his Passion, death, Resurrection, and glorious Ascension, Christ, the Savior of the world, has set us free.

The grace of God enables us to live in freedom, in the freedom of the children of God. By freely sacrificing his human life on the cross, Jesus won a people to himself. By shedding his blood, Jesus washed us clean from sin. By being raised from the dead, Christ provides us a way to do the same.

Through Baptism we receive the gift of **sanctifying grace**. Infused by

Life in the Holy Spirit

After Jesus ascended to his Father, the Father sent the Holy Spirit to accompany us down life's twisting paths. "Uniting us by faith and Baptism to the Passion and Resurrection of Christ, the Spirit makes us sharers in his life" (*Catechism of the Catholic Church* 2017). We are made holy again.

This work of the Holy Spirit is called **sanctification**. We can accept forgiveness and the gift of having our friendship with God restored. We can grow in our ability to make right choices and live as God's adopted children.

Our justification, our salvation in Christ, is the work of God's mercy. It has as its goal the glory of God and of Christ, and the gift of our eternal life with God.

What evidence can you offer that the Holy Spirit is at work in the world around you?

Sharing in the Life of Grace

Jesus tells a parable about an official who owed a huge debt to a king (see Matthew 18:21–35). When the official begged for mercy, the king forgave his whole debt.

The official in the Gospel parable did not merit the king's mercy. The word **merit** means "to be worthy of, deserve." Something we merit is something that we are entitled to or worthy of. It is a reward that we have earned because of certain tasks we have successfully accomplished. For example, students merit good grades because they study hard and successfully pass a course or test.

God owes us nothing. Every blessing, every grace we have, God freely gives us out of his love for us. How then can we talk about meriting God's free gifts of mercy, forgiveness, and salvation? No one can merit the initial grace that calls us back to God. We can only merit grace because God has chosen to allow us to share in his work of grace. Notice the word *share*.

Cooperating with the Holy Spirit, we can merit certain blessings and graces needed for living our life as children of God here on earth and for attaining eternal life in heaven. Cooperating with the Holy Spirit, we first seek the kingdom of God. Then all things will be given us besides (see Matthew 6:33).

Jesus' love is the source of all merit before God. God gives us his grace through his Son, whose love has won us everything. Jesus is the key to understanding the concepts of merit, grace, and justification. Meriting eternal life is first of all associated with the grace of God and, second, with our cooperation. By cooperating with the Holy Spirit, we merit the rewards God has prepared for us.

FAITH CONNECTION

Think of someone who has made a difference by cooperating with the grace of the Holy Spirit. Design a "merit badge" to honor this person. On these lines write a saying for the badge.

_____

_____

OUR CHURCH
MAKES A DIFFERENCE

The Parish Community

The Son of God took on flesh and became one of us so that we could share in the divine life of the Father, Son, and Holy Spirit. We cooperate with the grace of God as members of the Body of Christ and support one another in living as God's children. Catholics support one another in many ways. One important way is belonging to communities of faith called parishes.

A parish community is a part of the larger faith community called a diocese. There are more than nineteen thousand parishes in the United States of America. The spiritual leader of the parish is called a pastor. He is the coworker with the bishop, who is the leader of the diocese, or a particular Church.

Parishioners, or members of a parish, support one another in living their life in Christ in many ways. They celebrate the liturgy and sacraments. They share their faith through a wide variety of educational programs for children, youth, and adults. They work for peace and justice, bring comfort to the ill, share food and clothing with those experiencing financial difficulties, and pray with those grieving over the loss of a loved one. Parishioners share their time, talents, and treasures to build up the Body of Christ on earth and prepare the way for the coming of the kingdom of God.

In what ways does your parish show it is cooperating with the grace of God to build up the Church on earth?

WHAT DIFFERENCE
Does Faith Make in My Life?

"Response-Ability"

In this chapter you learned about the grace of the Holy Spirit and how grace is active in our lives. It is through prayer and the grace of the Holy Spirit that we are able to remain open and respond to God's goodness in others.

As a follower of Jesus you are asked to see God in all those you meet. We are all God's children and he dwells within each and every one of us. People from all different cultures—people who seem just like us and people who seem very different—are all children of God. God created and loves and cherishes each and every person.

Dignity

So what does that mean to you? What it means, and what the grace of the Holy Spirit enables us to do, is to respect the uniqueness of each person. Jesus spent a lot of time teaching about love and living the divine commandment to love.

You are to love others—without exception—just as Jesus did and commanded all his disciples to do. Your response of love is to acknowledge that every person is created and loved by God. Your responsibility is to treat every person with dignity and respect.

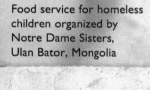

Food service for homeless children organized by Notre Dame Sisters, Ulan Bator, Mongolia

Homeless woman asleep on bench, Battery Park, New York City

How Can You Make a Difference?

When people are not willing to accept the responsibility of treating others with dignity and respect, the results can be horrendous. You have heard and read about violence, abuse, and hate crimes. These things happen when people think they have the right to hurt, torture, and even kill another person.

You can work to build attitudes that lead to love taught by Jesus. You can make a difference by:

- ⭐ remembering that God dwells in each person. Say to yourself whenever you see another human being, "It is the Lord." When you can make this a habit, you will find it easier to respect others.

- ⭐ looking for the goodness in others. God is not finished with any of us yet. We can all grow and change and become better people.

- ⭐ accepting people for who they are, especially if they are different from you.

- ⭐ affirming the positive qualities and characteristics of others and supporting them in the use of their gifts and talents.

- ⭐ doing random acts of kindness because you believe that people are worth it.

Physically challenged athlete and coach

Faith Decision

- Work in small groups. Imagine that you have been hired as the writers for a new TV series called *Do unto Others*. Each week the show will present a dilemma that is solved by people choosing to respect one another. Make up titles for the first four episodes.

- Choose one of the titles and outline the screenplay. Share your outline with the other groups.

Think of one thing you could begin doing this week that will show you believe that all people should be treated with dignity. Write what you will do here:

_____

_____

_____

PRAY and REVIEW

Prayer to the Holy Spirit

All: In the name of the Father, and of the Son, and of the Holy Spirit.

Leader: Let us pray to the Holy Spirit for the grace to live as faithful followers of Jesus.

Come, Holy Spirit, fill the hearts of your faithful and kindle in them the fire of your love.

Group 1: Help us honor all people as children of God and treat them with respect.

All: Holy Spirit, kindle in us the fire of your love.

Group 2: Open our hearts to your grace that we may treat others with kindness and generosity.

All: Holy Spirit, kindle in us the fire of your love.

Group 3: Teach us to work for peace and justice and to bring comfort to those who are suffering.

All: Holy Spirit, kindle in us the fire of your love.

Leader: God, our Father, send the Holy Spirit, to guide and teach us to renew the faith of the earth by living as your Son taught us. We ask this in his name.

All: Amen.

FAITH VOCABULARY

Define each of these faith terms:

1. grace
2. sanctifying grace
3. justification
4. sanctification
5. merit

MAIN IDEAS

Choose either (a) or (b) from each set of items. Write a brief paragraph to answer each of your choices.

1. (a) Describe how the parable of the Sower helps us understand grace.
   (b) Discuss the importance of freely responding to God's grace.

2. (a) Discuss how grace makes us alive in Christ.
   (b) Explain how we are made holy again through the Holy Spirit.

CRITICAL THINKING

Using what you have learned in this chapter, briefly explain this Scripture verse:

"[S]eek first the kingdom [of God] and his righteousness, and all these things will be given you besides."   MATTHEW 6:33

FAMILY DISCUSSION

How does our family show that we are cooperating with God's gift of grace to live as a Christian family?

For more ideas on ways your family can live your faith, visit the "Faith First for Families" page at **www.FaithFirst.com**. Also check out the latest games on the Teen Center.

A. The Best Response

Read each statement and circle the best answer.

1. What do we call the gift or power to know God and to reflect on how he is part of our lives?
   - A. free will
   - B. intellect
   - C. revelation
   - D. power

2. What is Christian morality?
   - A. the Passion, death, and Resurrection of Christ
   - B. the way of living for those who have been joined to Christ through Baptism
   - C. the way of life for a group of teenagers
   - D. the root of all morality

3. What is conscience?
   - A. a little man inside our heads
   - B. a persistent voice that helps us make choices
   - C. the Holy Spirit
   - D. our soul

4. What are the four cardinal virtues?
   - A. prudence, love, justice, and temperance
   - B. hope, charity, justice, and peace
   - C. prudence, justice, fortitude, and temperance
   - D. prudence, hope, charity, and peace

5. What does the goodness or evilness of an act depend on?
   - A. morality, virtues, and actions
   - B. object, intention, and circumstances
   - C. intentions, actions, and emotions
   - D. none of the above

B. Matching Words and Phrases

Match the terms in column A with the descriptions in column B.

Column A

_____ 1. Evangelists

_____ 2. sanctifying grace

_____ 3. actual grace

_____ 4. justification

_____ 5. social sin

_____ 6. merit

_____ 7. theological virtues

_____ 8. grace

_____ 9. Paschal Mystery

_____ 10. mortal sin

Column B

a. our personal participation in the life of the Trinity

b. divine help empowering us to live as children of God

c. inspired writers of the Gospel

d. deadly sin

e. faith, hope, charity

f. Passion, death, Resurrection, and glorious Ascension of Jesus Christ

g. abortion, mercy killing, poverty

h. making things right through Christ

i. to deserve

j. our participation in the very life of God

C. What I Have Learned

Using what you have learned in Unit One, write a two-sentence reflection about each of the following statements.

Jesus calls us to holiness and happiness.

_____

_____

Every society has a responsibility to be just.

_____

_____

D. A Scripture Story

Saint Paul the Apostle made an attempt to quiet conflict when he wrote about love to the early Church in Corinth. Write a reflection telling how Saint Paul's words can help resolve conflict in your school or community.

UNIT TWO
The Ten Commandments

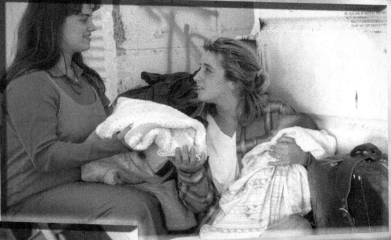

What is at the heart and center of the Law of God?

Getting Ready

The Law of God

What do you already know about the Ten Commandments and the Beatitudes?

The Ten Commandments

_____

_____

_____

The Beatitudes

_____

_____

_____

Questions I Have

What questions do you have about the moral teachings of the Catholic Church?

_____

_____

_____

_____

Faith Vocabulary

Put an X next to the faith vocabulary terms that you know. Put a ? next to the faith vocabulary terms that you need to know more about.

_____ Decalogue

_____ reverence

_____ idol

_____ obedience

_____ euthanasia

_____ chastity

_____ stewardship

_____ reparation

_____ covet

_____ avarice

_____ greed

_____ temptation

A Scripture Story

Jesus in the home of Martha and Mary

What do you know about what happened when Jesus visited the home of Martha and Mary?

The First, Second, and Third Commandments

7

FAITH FOCUS

How does God tell us how he wants us to live?

FAITH VOCABULARY

Decalogue

precepts

idols

reverence

Describe an experience of trying to find your way without clear directions to a place you had never been before.

Imagine a highway system with no road signs. Then imagine traveling across the country without a map. It might take a very long time to find your way from Maine to California!

During their wandering in the desert during the Exodus, things were not going well for the Israelites. Their journey to a life of freedom in the land God promised to them seemed to be going nowhere. Moses went up Mount Sinai, and God gave him and the Israelites the Ten Commandments.

How do the Ten Commandments give direction to our journey through life on earth?

"I have set before you life and death, the blessing and the curse. Choose life, then, that you and your descendants may live."

DEUTERONOMY 30:19

Choose God, Choose Life

The Gift of the Law of God

The Ten Commandments are also called the **Decalogue**, which means "ten words." They are God's gift to the Israelites and to all people. The Decalogue states the foundation of our life with God and with one another. In this sense the Ten Commandments are the traditional and time-tested measure of our character as human beings. They state **precepts** that all people have a serious obligation to obey.

The Law of the Human Heart

The Ten Commandments summarize the Law of God written on every human heart. This law is called the natural law. It is the foundation of all human laws, moral and civil. The Ten Commandments revealed by God give us a clearer picture of that law.

1. I am the LORD your God: you shall not have strange gods before me.
2. You shall not take the name of the LORD your God in vain.
3. Remember to keep holy the LORD's Day.
4. Honor your father and your mother.
5. You shall not kill.
6. You shall not commit adultery.
7. You shall not steal.
8. You shall not bear false witness against your neighbor.
9. You shall not covet your neighbor's wife.
10. You shall not covet your neighbor's goods.

Describe the connection between the natural law and the Ten Commandments.

Jesus and the Law

The revelation of the Law on Mount Sinai prepared for the revelation of Jesus Christ. Jesus, the Word of God, became flesh, and fulfilled the revelation of the old Law. Jesus taught his disciples:

> "Do not think that I have come to abolish the law or the prophets. I have come not to abolish but to fulfill. . . . [W]hoever obeys and teaches these commandments will be called greatest in the kingdom of heaven." MATTHEW 5:17, 19

Jesus called people to return to the way of their hearts—to love God and other people with their whole heart (see Matthew 22:37–39). Paul the Apostle states it simply:

> [L]ove is the fulfillment of the law. ROMANS 13:10

Jesus did not simply reveal the fulfillment of the Law. He also gave us the Holy Spirit to live the Law of God to its fullest. This New Testament prayer says it all:

> I kneel before the Father . . . that he may grant you . . . to be strengthened with power through his Spirit in the inner self, and that Christ may dwell in your hearts through faith; that you, rooted and grounded in love, may . . . know the love of Christ that surpasses knowledge, so that you may be filled with all the fullness of God. EPHESIANS 3:14, 16–19

Compare the Law of God revealed to Moses with the revelation of Jesus.

FAITH CONNECTION

Work with a group. Prepare a list of key rules that can help you live the Ten Commandments as Jesus taught. Then number your rules in order of their importance.

_____

_____

_____

_____

_____

The First Commandment

I am the LORD your God: you shall not have strange gods before me. BASED ON EXODUS 20:2–3

The First Commandment commands us to set our priorities straight. Our first priority in life is to acknowledge this truth: that God is God and that we are not. We are to believe in God, hope in God, and love God above all creatures.

The First Commandment is fairly straightforward: Put God first and worship him alone. In this day and age, the First Commandment is violated in many ways.

Atheism. Atheism is the rejection or denial of the existence of God.

Idolatry. Idolatry is worshiping **idols,** or false gods. An idol is anything that takes the place of God in our life. It is something that takes over our life.

Sacrilege. Sacrilege consists of mistreating anyone or anything that is set aside, or consecrated, for worshiping God or helping people live as children of God.

Superstition, divination, and magic. Superstition, divination, and magic divert us from trusting in God's loving providence by claiming "special powers" on our own.

Simony. Simony is the abuse of spiritual power for personal gain.

All these practices can undermine true religion and belief in God.

What is the heart and center of the First Commandment?

Spires of Saint Patrick's Cathedral, New York City, New York

The Second Commandment

You shall not take the name
of the LORD your God in vain.
EXODUS 20:7

Respecting a person's name is the same as respecting the person. The Israelites had the highest form of respect, or **reverence,** for God and the very name of God. So great was the Israelites' reverence for the name that God revealed to Moses that YHWH was not spoken aloud. Names such as "LORD" were substituted in place of YHWH.

Showing such reverence for God's name is showing reverence for God himself. For Christians reverence for the person and name of Jesus is the same.

God greatly exalted him
and bestowed on him the name
that is above every name,
that at the name of Jesus
every knee should bend,
of those in heaven and on
    earth and under the earth,
and every tongue confess that
Jesus Christ is Lord,
to the glory of God the Father.
PHILIPPIANS 2:9–11

Speaking the name of God, Jesus, Mary, the saints, or holy things in an offensive way is an act of irreverence. We call such acts of irreverence *blasphemy.* We also dishonor the name of God when we commit perjury. Perjury is the taking of a false oath by calling on God, who is Truth, to be a witness to a lie.

How would you summarize the meaning of the First and Second Commandments in one sentence?

Jesus Christ Is Lord

Holy Bible

Did you Know...

In the United States Catholics celebrate six holy days of obligation in addition to Sundays. They are Mary, Mother of God (January 1), Ascension of the Lord (the Thursday ten days before Pentecost, or the Sunday before Pentecost), the Assumption of Mary (August 15), All Saints' Day (November 1), Immaculate Conception of Mary (December 8), and Christmas (December 25).

The Third Commandment

Remember to keep holy the LORD's Day. BASED ON EXODUS 20:8

The Lord's Day is the day set aside to honor God. We keep the Lord's Day holy by acknowledging the primacy of our relationship with God. We worship God and re-create our proper relationship with God, with our family, with others, and with all creation. We use our time to make sure that no other demands prevent us from making the observance of the Lord's Day the center of our week. Every Christian also has the obligation to avoid making demands on others that prevent them from observing the Lord's Day.

For Christians Sunday is the Lord's Day. It commemorates Christ's Resurrection, which is the beginning of the new creation of all things in Christ. The Sunday Eucharistic liturgy is the heart of the Church's celebration of the Lord's Day. We join with Christ in unity with the Holy Spirit in praying the Church's great prayer of blessing and thanksgiving to God the Father and Creator. We remember and share in Christ's work of his re-creating all things new through the saving events of his Paschal Mystery. We receive the grace, the nourishment, and the strength to show our reverence for God in all our words and actions.

So vital is our joining with the whole Church in celebrating the Eucharist that the Church obliges us to participate in its celebration on Sundays and other holy days of obligation. We can no more do without the spiritual nourishment of hearing the word of God and sharing in the Eucharist on a regular basis than we can do without the physical nourishment of food and drink.

FAITH · CONNECTION

Create and illustrate an announcement proclaiming Sunday as the Lord's Day. Write the words of your announcement in this space.

_____

_____

_____

OUR CHURCH MAKES A DIFFERENCE

The Precepts of the Church

The Decalogue, or Ten Commandments, states the foundation of our life with God and with one another. The First, Second, and Third Commandments guide us in living our relationship with God.

The Church has given Catholics some practical ways to live out our relationship with God. These are called the precepts of the Church. The Catechism lists these precepts:

* You shall attend Mass on Sundays and on holy days of obligation and rest from servile labor.
* You shall confess your sins at least once a year.
* You shall receive the sacrament of the Eucharist at least during the Easter season.
* You shall observe the days of fasting and abstinence established by the Church.
* You shall help to provide for the needs of the Church.

We also have the responsibility of providing for the material needs of the Church according to our ability.

Catechism of the Catholic Church 2042–2043

The precepts of the Church guide us in worshiping God and showing our reverence for him in all we say and do. They guide us in acknowledging that God is God, in trusting and loving him above all creatures, and in placing all our hopes in him.

How do the precepts of the Church guide you in living the Ten Commandments?

WHAT DIFFERENCE
Does Faith Make in My Life?

False Gods

In this chapter you learned about the First, Second, and Third Commandments. These three Commandments teach us how to live our relationship with God. These Commandments tell us how to love God, how to always put him first in our lives, and how to honor and worship him through our words and actions. The First Commandment reminds us to love, praise, and adore God above everyone and everything. We are called to remember that there is only one God who is to be the center of our lives, and that no other "false gods," such as power or material things, should ever come before him.

In our society you hear slogans that claim "more is better" and "much wants more." Advertisements bombard you with promises that if you wear "our brand of whatever," you will have power, prestige, fame, money—you will be "number one."

As a young person, what false gods are you encouraged to choose as number one in your life? When you are faced with a hard decision, how can you choose God, true values, and your religious beliefs over the following?

* money
* power
* video games
* sports
* sports heroes
* music stars
* music videos
* popularity
* sex
* designer clothes
* language
* beauty products
* models

How can you choose name-brand things, or choose to belong to a certain group, and not allow them to rule your life?

Faith Decision

Discuss with your small group one of the following scenarios.

* Your friends are going to a rock concert of your favorite group. Your parents have forbidden you to listen to this group because their lyrics and actions promote drugs, violence, and sexual activity. Your parents tell you that you cannot go to this concert. You want to fit in with your group. What do you do?

* Your favorite sports team is in the playoffs for the first time ever. The game will be broadcast at 10:00 A.M. on Sunday. This is the only time you can have transportation for Mass. What will you do?

This week I will put God first in my life. I will

_____

_____

_____

_____

_____ .

PRAY and REVIEW

The Divine Praises

The Divine Praises are a prayer of blessing and adoration. A prayer of blessing and adoration acknowledges that we are creatures, exalts the Creator who made us, and recognizes that God is the source of all that is good.

Group 1: Blessed be God.
Group 2: Blessed be his holy name.

Group 1: Blessed be Jesus Christ, true God and true man.
Group 2: Blessed be the name of Jesus.

Group 1: Blessed be his most Sacred Heart.
Group 2: Blessed be his most precious Blood.

Group 1: Blessed be Jesus in the most holy Sacrament of the altar.
Group 2: Blessed be the Holy Spirit, the Paraclete.

Group 1: Blessed be the great Mother of God, Mary most holy.
Group 2: Blessed be her holy and Immaculate Conception.

Group 1: Blessed be her glorious Assumption.
Group 2: Blessed be the name of Mary, Virgin and Mother.

Group 1: Blessed be Saint Joseph, her most chaste spouse.
Group 2: Blessed be God in his angels and in his saints.

FAITH VOCABULARY

Define each of these faith words:

1. Decalogue
2. precepts
3. idols
4. reverence

MAIN IDEAS

Choose either (a) or (b) from each set of items. Write a brief paragraph to answer each of your choices.

1. (a) Describe the Ten Commandments as a summary of God's Law.
   (b) Why is the First Commandment the foundation of the other Commandments?

2. (a) What is the connection between reverence and the Second Commandment?
   (b) Describe the importance of taking part in the celebration of the Eucharist on Sunday.

CRITICAL THINKING

Using what you have learned in this chapter, briefly explain this statement:
   The Ten Commandments summarize the Law of God written on every human heart.

FAMILY DISCUSSION

Why is showing reverence for one another important in the life of a family?

For more ideas on ways your family can live your faith, visit the "Faith First for Families" page at **www.FaithFirst.com**. Also the chapter review in the Teen Center will help you review what you have learned this week.

Martha and Mary
A Scripture Story

8

Jesus, Martha, and Mary, detail from bronze door. Otto Lessing (1812–1901), German painter/sculptor.

FAITH FOCUS

Why did Jesus spend time with his friends?

FAITH VOCABULARY

disciple

What do you do to help your friendships grow stronger?

A sure sign of friendship is spending time together. We do not talk with anyone else the way we talk with our friends, especially our closest friends. Our friends are often the first to know about both the things that bring us joy and happiness as well as the things that bring us sadness and suffering.

The Gospel writers give us many examples of Jesus spending time with his closest friends, his disciples. Those were moments when Jesus would take time to teach them about being his disciples.

What Gospel stories do you know about Jesus spending time with his friends?

Mary . . . sat beside the Lord at his feet listening to him speak.
LUKE 10:39

Women Disciples of Jesus

At the time of Jesus' life on earth, it was a common practice among Jewish, Greek, and Roman people for a teacher to attract and have disciples. The word *disciple* has its roots in two Latin words—*discere* which means "to learn" and *discipulus* which means "a pupil." A **disciple** is a person who learns from another person and follows and spreads the teachings of that person. The disciples of Jesus, whom they respectfully addressed as Rabbi, or Teacher, did just that (see John 1:38).

In Jesus' time, only men customarily were able to become disciples of such a teacher. It would have been out of the ordinary for a teacher to have spoken to women publicly, explain his teachings to them, and invite them to become his disciples as Jesus did. But in the Gospels we read that both women and men are numbered among the disciples of Jesus.

Qualities of Discipleship

Reading the many Gospel passages that focus on Jesus and his women disciples reveals many of the qualities of a true disciple of Christ.

Faith and Trust

Discipleship demands faith and trust. The widow of Nain (see Luke 7:11–17), the sinful woman whom Jesus forgave (see Luke 7:36–50), and Martha and Mary (see John 11:1–27) exemplify those qualities. As the widow of Nain, the sinful woman, and Martha and Mary did, we need to place ourselves in Jesus' presence in our moments of need and, with trust and faith, share our situation with him.

Jesus Teaching at the Seashore. James J. Tissot (1836–1902), French painter.

Raising of the Widow's Son. James J. Tissot.

Prayerful Listening

Discipleship demands prayerful listening. Jesus invited the Samaritan woman whom he met at Jacob's well into serious conversation (see John 4:4–42). She prayerfully listened and responded and had a change of heart.

Disciples of Jesus must spend time with him. He comes to us and welcomes us anytime and anyplace. We must honestly open our minds and hearts to him as the Samaritan woman did. We must listen as he replies. The more we engage in prayerful conversation with him, the more we will come to know him better and grow as his disciples.

Woman of Samaria at the Well.
James J. Tissot.

Confidence

Discipleship demands confidence in Jesus' love and concern for us. Jesus met many people and quite often visited them in their homes. We know that when Jesus and his disciples were near the village of Bethany, they often stayed at the home of Mary, Martha, and Lazarus. What an honor this must have been! Martha and Mary reached out to Jesus with confidence when Lazarus, their brother, died. With Jesus at our side, we can face even the most difficult of situations. He is always there with us.

Describe some of the qualities of a disciple of Jesus that we learn from the women disciples of Jesus.

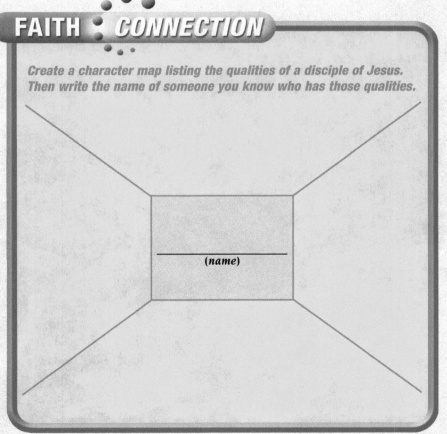

FAITH CONNECTION

Create a character map listing the qualities of a disciple of Jesus. Then write the name of someone you know who has those qualities.

(name)

Martha and Mary

Jesus and his disciples spent much time together traveling from village to village. On one of their journeys to Jerusalem, they passed through the village of Bethany and visited the home of Martha and Mary and Lazarus. This is what happened:

As they continued their journey he entered a village where a woman whose name was Martha welcomed him. She had a sister named Mary [who] sat beside the Lord at his feet listening to him speak. Martha, burdened with much serving, came to him and said, "Lord, do you not care that my sister has left me by myself to do the serving? Tell her to help me." The Lord said to her in reply, "Martha, Martha, you are anxious and worried about many things. There is need of only one thing. Mary has chosen the better part and it will not be taken from her." LUKE 10:38–42

Woman on road to Bethany in Israel. Bethany is on the eastern slope of the Mount of Olives about one and one-half miles from Jerusalem. It is now called Azariyeh, or "the place of Lazarus."

Luke's account of the Gospel begins and ends in the Temple of Jerusalem. One of the literary devices Luke uses to organize his account of the Gospel is Jesus' journey to Jerusalem (see Luke 9:51–19:27). It is during this part of the Gospel that Luke includes Jesus' teachings on the meaning of discipleship.

Martha and Mary with Jesus, mosaic. Artist unknown.

The story of Jesus visiting the home of Martha and Mary is found in chapter 10 of Luke's Gospel. Luke begins chapter 10 with Jesus teaching his disciples. Their work was to be carried out in his name. Luke then turns to the qualities and characteristics of that work. Living the Great Commandment (see Luke 10:25–28) is the foundation of Christian discipleship as the parable of the Good Samaritan clearly teaches (see Luke 10:29–37).

Luke next presents Jesus teaching Martha and Mary about the meaning of discipleship. What is the relationship between serving others and spending time alone listening to Jesus? Jesus invited these two sisters to consider exactly what their priorities were. Those who listen come away changed.

What did Jesus want Martha to understand about being his disciple?

MARY HATH CHOSEN THE BETTER PART

Understanding the Word of God

Jesus. Mary, on the other hand, is the reflective disciple. She spends her time sitting by the side of Jesus, listening and taking to heart his every word.

True Christian discipleship is a blend of both responses. When Martha complained about Mary's lack of service, Jesus replied:

"Martha, Martha, you are anxious and worried about many things. There is need of only one thing. Mary has chosen the better part and it will not be taken from her."

LUKE 10:41–42

Two Disciples— Two Different Approaches

This story suggests that Mary and Martha each had a somewhat different approach to being Jesus' disciple.

Martha is an example of an outgoing disciple who seems to thrive on serving

Our service needs to be founded on prayerful listening to the word of God.

The foundation of Christian discipleship is learning from the Teacher, Jesus. Disciples of Jesus first must listen to the word of Jesus.

Good works and service must flow from our listening to the word of God. We must prayerfully reflect on it and make it part of our lives. No matter how busy we become it is necessary that we hear and listen to the word of God. Only then can we live in loving service to others.

FAITH CONNECTION

Describe ways you sometimes are like both Mary and Martha.

Mary	Martha
_____	_____
_____	_____
_____	_____
_____	_____

The Liturgy of the Hours

The early Church gathered to pray in the morning and continued praying throughout the day. Morning and evening prayer became the normal daily liturgy, or public worship and work of the Church. Christian discipleship is a balance of prayer (Mary) and service (Martha).

Joining with the whole Church and praying the Liturgy of the Hours can help us maintain that balance in our lives. The Liturgy of the Hours is the public prayer of the Church. The Church today encourages the entire Christian community to gather for daily prayer. The Liturgy of the Hours consists of:

◆ **Lauds, or Morning Prayer,** which is celebrated at daybreak.

◆ **Daytime Prayer,** which is a short prayer said anytime throughout the day.

◆ **Vespers, or Evening Prayer,** which is celebrated in the early evening when the sun is setting.

◆ **Compline, or Night Prayer,** which is the prayer of the Church that marks the end of the day.

◆ **Office of Readings,** which can be prayed anytime throughout the day. It is a prayer containing biblical readings and excerpts of writings and sermons of the early Church.

Praying throughout the day helps us spend time with Jesus. It helps us set aside a time to listen to the word of God. This gives direction to our lives of service.

How can you set aside time throughout the day to spend time in prayer?

WHAT DIFFERENCE
Does Faith Make in My Life?

Prayer | Action

Balancing Prayer and Action

Service to others and prayer are both loving signs of disciples. An old saying tells us that "you cannot give what you do not have." The balance that we try to find is to spend some time in prayer so we can fill ourselves with God's love and listen to his message. This prayer time then fills us up with the courage and strength and the motivation to go out and do good works and be of service to others.

How Can We Pray?

The Church teaches us that there are five forms of prayer: blessing and adoration, praise, thanksgiving, petition, and intercession. We use all of these forms of prayer in the liturgy.

Blessing and Adoration

This form of prayer declares and acknowledges that God is the Creator and we are creatures. God the Creator is the source of all that is good. We bless and adore God who created us.

Petition

Prayers of petition ask God to give us the grace and help we need in our daily lives. We ask and trust God to provide for us, to give us what we ask for, and to take care of us. These prayers help us place our needs before God and help us listen for answers to some very important questions, such as: Lord Jesus, how do you want me to live my life? How do you want me to serve others? Help me understand what is going on in my life right now.

Intercession

This form of prayer helps us become aware of the needs of others. We ask God to bless, heal, or take care of those who are in need of his help and guidance.

Thanksgiving

Christians are a "people of thanks." Being thankful is synonymous with being a disciple of Christ. Saint Paul the Apostle teaches us "In all circumstances give thanks, for this is the will of God in Christ Jesus for you" (1 Thessalonians 5:18).

Praise

Our prayer of praise acknowledges that God is God. It gives glory beyond what he does and simply because he is God.

Let's Put These Prayers into Practice

As you learned from the story of Martha and Mary, Jesus calls you to balance and blend your prayer life with your loving actions. Every day you have an opportunity to do this. Whenever you see or hear of a tragedy—an earthquake, a tornado, a fire, a flood, fatal car accidents, senseless shootings—you hear about people who stepped forward to be of service. But there are many other opportunities too. Here are some suggestions:

✳ Donate your time to help clean up or rebuild someone's home.
✳ Give good used clothing, shoes, toys, or household things to those in need.
✳ As a family, donate food to disaster victims or to food banks.
✳ Use a portion of your own money to help someone who has less than you.

Look for opportunities in your own family, school, and neighborhood to help others who may need a helping hand, a listening ear, or a supportive shoulder to lean on. Pray for those in need.

Faith Decision

Discuss ways to balance prayer and action in your life.

This week I will set aside _____ as a time of prayer. I can reach out to someone in need by

_____

_____

_____

_____.

Write your two ideas on note cards and keep them in a place where they will remind you of your decisions.

PRAY and REVIEW

Love and Serve the Lord

Leader: God, heavenly Father,
you sent us your Son,
the Word of God made flesh.
Send us the Holy Spirit
to teach and guide us
to listen and to follow the life
and teachings of your Son.

Reader: A reading from the book
of the prophet Isaiah.
(Proclaim Isaiah 58:6–9.)
The word of the Lord.

All: **Thanks be to God.**

Leader: Let us ask our Lord Jesus
Christ to help us follow
his example of prayer
and service.

Group 1: Lord, Jesus Christ,
you went off alone to be
with your Father in prayer.

All: **Teach us to follow you.**

Group 2: From your birth to your
death you manifested a total
self-surrender to your Father.

All: **Teach us to follow you.**

Group 1: You proclaimed that you
came to serve and not
to be served.

All: **Teach us to follow you.**

Group 2: Your whole life was given
in service both to your
Father and to others.

All: **Teach us to follow you.**
(Offer one another a sign
of peace.)

FAITH VOCABULARY

Use the term *disciple* correctly in a sentence.

MAIN IDEAS

Choose either (a) or (b) from each set of items. Write a brief paragraph to answer each of your choices.

1. (a) Describe some of the qualities of a true disciple of Jesus that women in the Gospel teach us.
   (b) Describe what Martha and Mary do during Jesus' visit to their home. Explain Jesus' response to Martha's request.

2. (a) Compare how Martha and Mary are both examples of disciples of Jesus.
   (b) Explain the importance of Jesus' disciples prayerfully listening to him.

CRITICAL THINKING

Using what you have learned in this chapter, briefly explain this Scripture verse:
"Mary has chosen the better part." LUKE 10:42

FAMILY DISCUSSION

What is the relationship between prayer and service within our family?

For more ideas on ways your family can live your faith, visit the "Faith First for Families" page at **www.FaithFirst.com**. Also check out the Teen Center to discover this week's saint.

The Fourth and Fifth Commandments

9

FAITH FOCUS

How do we respect and strengthen our life as a family?

FAITH VOCABULARY

obedience

direct abortion

euthanasia

Who are the most elderly members of your family? What does your family do to show respect for them?

By 2020, the U.S. Census Bureau projects that there will be more than sixty million Americans between the ages of 65 and 74. In 1900 there were only 3.1 million. The aging of the U.S. population raises many issues related to the Fourth and Fifth Commandments. These issues include respect and care for the elderly and a variety of end-of-life issues.

How do you follow Jesus' commandment to "love one another"?

Through all generations your truth endures.
PSALM 119:90

93

Honoring and Obeying

The Fourth Commandment

Honor your father and your mother. Exodus 20:12

With this Commandment, which follows the Commandments that describe our relationship with God, God calls our attention to our whole family, including its elderly members. Our family is the most important community to which we belong. It is the heart and center of all other communities.

Cooperating with God our Father and Creator, parents share the gift of life with children. It is the parents' duty to provide as far as possible for the physical and spiritual needs of their children. By word and example, Christian parents teach their children that the first calling of the Christian is to follow Christ. They respect and encourage and support their children's vocations.

Children often think of the Fourth Commandment as "obeying" their parents. What does *obey* really mean?

Obedience includes the respectful listening and trusting response to a person who has authority over us and asks us to do something that is in accordance with God's Law and a just civil law.

When we obey the commands of our parents and trust in their guidance, we show the esteem in which we hold them. When we listen with respect, respond to their guidance with trust, and support them in their old age, we honor them. We build harmony in our families and strengthen the bonds that hold us together as a family.

God is quite clear. He lays down the law: After him we are to honor and obey our parents, guardians, and those people who have the responsibility and authority for our growth and well-being.

Explain the relationship between obeying your parents and honoring them.

The Civic Community

Civil authorities and citizens have responsibilities toward one another too. Civil authorities are those people who exercise legitimate authority in cities or towns and countries.

Civil authorities and citizens are to work together to build just and compassionate communities. These tasks and responsibilities include:

- respecting all human life as sacred.
- respecting that the rights of people flow from their dignity as persons created by God.
- protecting and fostering the human rights of all citizens without exception.
- guaranteeing conditions that promote and protect human life and freedom, and the peace and safety of all people.
- working to alleviate the sinful inequalities that exist between people.
- guarding against the dangers of a totalitarian society. A totalitarian society is a society in which one group of people exercises absolute control over everyone and uses falsehood and violence to silence opposition.

Civil authorities sometime establish and enforce laws and policies that go against these principles. Our responsibility as citizens who are disciples of Christ is to work to change sinful and destructive policies. As the word of God teaches, "We must obey God rather than men" (Acts of the Apostles 5:29).

As citizens we honor and respect civil authorities by (1) working with them in a spirit of truth and justice, (2) loving and serving and defending our country, and (3) paying taxes, exercising our right to vote, and serving on juries.

FAITH : CONNECTION

Imagine that you will take part in a state Senate session. What issues would you want to raise about your age group? What solutions would you propose?

_____

_____

_____

The Fifth Commandment

You shall not kill.   EXODUS 20:13

The Fifth Commandment demands that we respect and protect the sacredness of human life.

God is the author of life. He creates every human person in his image and likeness. He shares his life and love with every person without exception. Without God's decision to share himself, there would be no created life—no thing, no person would exist. We are to honor and respect all human life as sacred.

God's command to respect all human life as sacred is violated in many ways. Violence in many forms has become part of the story of our life. The Fifth Commandment calls us to stand against violence. It condemns and forbids the evils and grave sins that do violence to human life. These include:

Murder. Murder is the direct and intentional killing of an innocent person. In all its forms murder is always gravely sinful. Even cooperating in such an act as an accomplice is a sin.

Abortion. A child who is conceived but not yet born is to be treated as a person. **Direct abortion**, or the direct and intentional killing of an unborn child, is always gravely contrary to the moral law. It violates the dignity of the human person and the holiness of the Creator.

Marchers walking in front of Supreme Court building during a pro-life rally in Washington, D.C.

Suicide. Suicide is the intentional and direct killing of oneself. When a personal friend or member of a family commits suicide, the survivors experience overwhelming sadness and pain. Unanswered questions about the salvation of our loved ones arise. We believe and trust that God in loving mercy and forgiveness reaches out to those who take their own lives. Most often they are not completely free because of some illness or serious mental disease. In that case they are not fully responsible for their action.

Euthanasia. **Euthanasia** is the direct and intentional killing of a person who is suffering from a long-term or even terminal illness. Some people mistakenly believe that administering lethal drugs or helping suffering people administer lethal drugs to themselves is an act of mercy and compassion. The Church teaches that mercy killing is murder. It violates the dignity of the human person and the respect due to God, who is the author of life.

Describe why direct abortion, suicide, and euthanasia are gravely wrong.

Pro-life rally on the National Mall near the Washington Monument, Washington, D.C.

PUBLIC HEARING
on
EUTHANASIA

People taking part in a meeting on euthanasia at the European Parliament in Strasbourg, France

Violent Lifestyles

We show respect for the gift of our own lives by living healthy lifestyles. Harmful or life-threatening behaviors, on the other hand, are acts of violence. They are against the sacredness of life and our dignity as persons.

We live responsibly when we do not abuse prescription drugs, over-the-counter drugs, or alcohol. Drugs, including nicotine, are among the leading killers or accomplices in the death of both young people and adults. We defend human life when we stand against the use and selling of illegal drugs, such as cocaine and heroin.

We respect the gift of our life when we eat, exercise, and care for our health responsibly. A proper diet is necessary. People also abuse their bodies through serious eating disorders characterized by a fear of weight gain leading to faulty eating habits, malnutrition, and excessive weight loss. Some athletes use steroids to build up muscles and strength. While this may lead to some initial strength benefits, it

also results in lifetime losses for the human body. The abuse of steroids is a violation of the Fifth Commandment. So serious is this popular practice that athletes who use them are routinely declared ineligible to participate.

Unjust anger, hatred, prejudice, and the desire for revenge can easily lead to acts of violence against human life. Domestic violence, hate crimes, road rage, and shootings in schools and in workplaces are but a few examples of how such feelings and attitudes can lead to violent acts against others.

FAITH : CONNECTION

Imagine that you are teaching a class to inform young people about choices that show respect for their bodies and for one another. Decide on topics and key points for three sessions. Jot down the theme of each session here:

Session 1: _____

Session 2: _____

Session 3: _____

OUR CHURCH MAKES A DIFFERENCE

Choosing Peace

The values of the Gospel and the values of society for resolving issues are sometimes in conflict. Proclaiming the Gospel in such situations is not an easy task. When this happens, the Church stands firm and speaks boldly. It does not cave in to the pressure of popular values that go against the Gospel proclaimed by Jesus. Some of the challenges to peace in our time are:

Self-defense. There is little doubt about both our personal right and obligation to defend ourselves and society's right and obligation to legitimately defend its citizens against the actions of an unjust aggressor. Exercising this right, however, is not always easy. There are limits to the ways we can defend ourselves. We are limited to using only the force necessary to protect ourselves. Taking someone's life who is trying to steal our sneakers, for example, is not self-protection.

Capital punishment. Executing people as punishment for certain crimes is called capital punishment. While the Catholic Church allows for capital punishment in very limited circumstances, it teaches that society should rarely, if ever, use the death penalty.

War. Waging war is perhaps humankind's most horrific act of violence. It is always a great evil. War paradoxically defends the sacredness of life and human freedom by destroying human life. Because of the evils and injustices war brings with it, the Church demands that we must do everything reasonably possible to avoid it. Should war occur all combatants must adhere to the principles of the moral law. We must never forget that every human life is sacred. All war crimes demand reparation.

Military strategists believe that one way to prevent war is to create and stockpile weapons of mass destruction. The Church, however, seriously questions this practice and describes it as "one of the greatest curses on the human race and the harm it inflicts on the poor is more than can be endured" (*Pastoral Constitution on the Church in the Modern World*, 81).

Give examples of people or groups who strive to solve conflicts peacefully without using violence.

99

WHAT DIFFERENCE
Does Faith Make in My Life?

Violence Versus Peace

In this chapter you learned that violence and disregard for human life can cause pain and unnecessary suffering. The Fifth Commandment call us to be peace-filled people.

Have you ever seen, heard, or been in any of these situations?

* Bang, boom, crash, boom! You hear these and other deafening sounds of video games blowing up skeletal people, shooting aliens, and firing missiles.
* Your brother or sister used your shirt without asking. You find it rolled up and dirty, thrown on the floor. You start yelling.
* Two men get out of their cars and start cursing and pushing one another.
* You turn on your TV and hear the news of another school shooting in which innocent people were killed and injured.

Violence in Homes, Schools, and Society

Violence is a very powerful and destructive force. Some people grow up thinking that violence is the only way to handle disagreements. They think that violent behavior is normal and an acceptable way to handle conflict. In your heart you know that using violence is not an acceptable way to handle conflict. Using violence to solve problems only begets more violence. We need to find peace-filled solutions to solving problems and handling our differences. As a Christian, you are called to be a person of peace, a peacemaker in conflict situations.

Terminator or Perpetuator

The word *terminator* at first seems to only have a violent meaning. The word literally means "one who puts an end to, or puts a stop to something." The word *perpetuator*, on the other hand, means "one who causes something to continue indefinitely." We all need to be terminators of violence and perpetuators of peace. Here are a few steps to help you be the terminator of violence and the perpetuator of peaceful problem solving.

Hands Shaking as Two People Watch. Lisa Henderling, contemporary artist/illustrator.

1. Stop

Keep your hands to yourself. Name what you are feeling. Anger and embarrassment usually cause an explosive reaction. You may feel powerless or resentful. Most people do not like these feelings so they try acting violently to get back their power or control. Cool down; pushing or hitting is not an acceptable way to solve the problem. Stop blaming the other person.

2. Look

Look at what happened. Were you embarrassed because of what happened? Were you mad because things didn't go your way? Focus on the facts of the situation. Can you accept your part of what happened?

3. Listen

Can you both look at the situation and think of another solution besides violence? Ask each other what would be the best way to peacefully settle this conflict.

4. Negotiate

What do you have to do to make things better? Negotiate the best solution. Be willing to compromise.

5. Evaluate

Evaluate the way you handle each problem. If you are too assertive, you may be pushy and selfish. When you are too compromising, you may be a pushover or be exploited by others. Decide if a peace-filled action solved the problem. If it did not, you may need to go back and repeat steps one through four.

Two Hands Forming Heart. José Ortega, contemporary artist/illustrator.

Faith Decision

- Many schools are adopting zero-tolerance policies about drugs, smoking, and physical fighting. Choose one of these issues and discuss three reasons in favor of and three reasons opposed to such a policy.

- What can you personally do to be a peaceful problem solver at home or in school? Write what you will do here.

_____

_____

_____

_____

_____

_____

PRAY and REVIEW

Prayer for Peace

Leader:
Lord, make me an instrument of your peace:

Group 1:
where there is hatred, let me sow love; where there is injury, pardon;

Group 2:
where there is doubt, faith; where there is despair, hope;

Group 1:
where there is darkness, light; where there is sadness, joy.

Group 2:
O Divine Master, grant that I may not so much seek to be consoled as to console,

Group 1:
to be understood as to understand, to be loved as to love.

Group 2:
For it is in giving that we receive, it is in pardoning that we are pardoned,

All:
and it is in dying that we are born to eternal life.

FAITH VOCABULARY

Use each of these terms correctly in a sentence.

1. obedience
2. direct abortion
3. euthanasia

MAIN IDEAS

Choose either (a) or (b) from each set of items. Write a brief paragraph to answer each of your choices.

1. (a) Describe why honoring and obeying our parents and civil authorities is at the heart of living the Fourth Commandment.
   (b) Explain why living the Fourth Commandment builds strong families and strong civil communities.

2. (a) Explain why all human life is sacred.
   (b) Describe how the Fifth Commandment helps us respect the sacredness of our own life and the lives of others.

CRITICAL THINKING

Using what you have learned in this chapter, briefly explain this Beatitude:
"Blessed are the peacemakers, / for they will be called children of God."   MATTHEW 5:9

FAMILY DISCUSSION

What are some of the ways we show our respect for one another?

For more ideas on ways your family can live your faith, visit the "Faith First for Families" page at **www.FaithFirst.com**. Also check out "Make a Difference" on the Teen Center.

The Sixth, Seventh, and Ninth Commandments

10

FAITH FOCUS

How do the Sixth and Ninth Commandments guide us in respecting ourselves and others?

FAITH VOCABULARY

chastity   reparation

stewardship

Who are some married couples you know who set a good example for young people? Tell why you chose them.

Men and women marry because they love each other and wish to form a family. By celebrating the sacrament of Matrimony, they also agree to dedicate themselves to the service of the Church. They serve as models of faithfulness and stewardship within their families and in their communities. They guide their children in developing strong moral values.

What do the Ten Commandments teach us about stewardship?

Love justice . . . ; think of the LORD in goodness, and seek him in integrity of heart.
WISDOM 1:1

Respecting Oneself and Others

The Sixth and Ninth Commandments

You shall not commit adultery. Exodus 20:14

You shall not covet your neighbor's wife. Exodus 20:17

The Sixth and Ninth Commandments guide us in suitably and properly expressing the gift of our human sexuality. They guide us to respect our own relationships and the relationships of other people.

Sexuality is the gift of being a man or a woman, a boy or a girl. Through our sexuality we express and share our life and love most intimately with and for others. These principles will guide us in using the gift of sexuality wisely according to God's plan:

- **Sexual identity.** Men and women need to acknowledge and accept their sexual identities.

- **Respect and honor your sexuality and the sexuality of others.** Women and men possess differences that balance and complete each other. When they honor one another, respect one another's gifts, and work together as suitable partners, they are images of the beauty and goodness of God. When women and men use these differences as a source of power to dominate one another, God's plan of creation itself is shown disrespect.

- **Aspire to a faithful marriage.** The only proper place for intimate sexual activity is within a lifelong marriage between a man and a woman.

- **Avoid sexual activity performed outside of marriage.** Adultery, fornication, premarital sex—even for an engaged couple, living together, a trial marriage, homosexual practices, and masturbation are not a part of God's plan for human sexuality.

These sins are gravely contrary to **chastity**. All erode our own value and the value of others.

- **Resist cultural pressures.** Music and television sitcoms, movies and videos, magazine articles, advertisements, and Internet sites routinely glamorize free, unlimited sex. These sexual relations are contrary to the Gospel.

- **Beware of fantasizing about another person.** Fantasizing may lead to coveting. In the Ninth Commandment *covet* means "desire another person, married or unmarried, for our own personal sexual pleasure." Acting immodestly may also lead to coveting.

- **Practice chastity.** Everyone is obliged to live a chaste life. The virtue of chastity guides us in expressing our sexuality properly according to our state in life. Married couples are to be open to God's gift of children. They are not to prevent the conception of a child by contraception or sterilization. Chastity involves the persistent habit of self-mastery and the controlling of our passions. Christ is the model for living a chaste life. All who are baptized into Christ receive the grace of the Holy Spirit to live a chaste life.

- **Practice temperance and modesty.** Temperance is the virtue that helps us respond appropriately to our desire to love and be loved. Modesty is decency. It protects who we are and our love. Modesty is the virtue that encourages patience and moderation in living out our friendships and loving relationships with others.

FAITH CONNECTION

Imagine that you are asked to prepare a photo article for a teen magazine showing young people living the Sixth Commandment. Describe two pictures your article would feature.

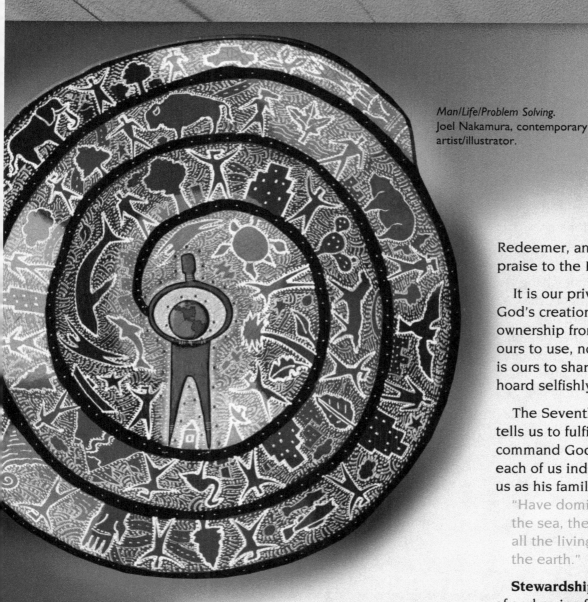

Man/Life/Problem Solving.
Joel Nakamura, contemporary
artist/illustrator.

Redeemer, and gives glory and praise to the Father.

It is our privilege to care for God's creation and not to usurp its ownership from God. Creation is ours to use, not to abuse. Creation is ours to share generously, not to hoard selfishly.

The Seventh Commandment tells us to fulfill responsibly the command God the Creator gave to each of us individually and to all of us as his family:

"Have dominion over the fish of the sea, the birds of the air, and all the living things that move on the earth."   Genesis 1:28

Stewardship is the managing of and caring for the property of another person. The stewardship of God's creation involves these concerns:

- **Concern for the future.** God gave us the whole world for everyone's use. We are to use it wisely and unselfishly. We are to use it and enjoy it, keeping others in mind. We are not to consume its resources for our own generation's profit and comfort. This impoverishes future generations and, in effect, steals from them.

The Seventh Commandment

You shall not steal.   Exodus 20:15

This commandment teaches that all creation belongs first of all to God the Creator. He is the source of all life, everything seen and unseen. Second, God created the world for the benefit of all. God has made us stewards of creation. Through our work we participate in the very work of God the Creator. Because we are joined to Christ in Baptism, our work is united to Christ, the

Animals are God's creatures. They belong to the household of God. While it is legitimate to responsibly use them for food and clothing, it is wrong to abuse them. We violate our responsibility as God's stewards when we cause animals to suffer or die needlessly.

- **Concern for the poor.** We serve Christ when we share our blessings with people in need (see Matthew 25:31–46). Good stewards act justly. They do not work merely to amass more and more wealth and property for their own good at the expense of others. Sharing acts are works of justice that are pleasing to God. The Church has a preferential love for those who are oppressed by poverty. The Church labors around the world to relieve, defend, and liberate the oppressed.

- **Concern for the common good.** We are a global family. God's children live all over the world. By reaching out to people in need, wherever they live, we are fulfilling our responsibility to act justly as stewards of God's creation.

- **Concern for public life.** We have a responsibility to take an active part in public life. We are to share our material blessings and our talents with others. Failure to vote, failure to contribute time for public service, and failure to lend our voices to matters of justice and the welfare of fellow citizens essentially rob society of our gifts and talents.

Why is it everyone's responsibility to relieve global starvation, poverty, and disease?

Stealing

The Seventh Commandment commands that we treat people justly. Stealing is an act of injustice. It is the taking or abusing of the possessions that rightfully and legitimately belong to another person. The word *possessions* in this description includes much more than the things people actually have. Here are some examples of stealing.

- Wage earners who are not given a fair and just wage for their work.
- The deliberate withholding of a lost item by a person who is not the original owner.
- The willful damage of what belongs to another.
- Cheating on a test, or taking another's knowledge and claiming it as our own.
- Discrimination in employment because of gender or religion or disability or immigrant status or sexual orientation.
- Increasing the profits and power of a few individuals at the expense of others and the whole human community.
- Slavery, which robs human beings of their freedom and reduces God's children to the status of merchandise.

All forms of stealing are acts of disrespect for the dignity of human beings. They are acts of injustice that demand **reparation.**

If we steal something, we must return it! If we have unjustly taken possession of another person's goods, we are required to give them back. If we have damaged those goods, we must offer to repair the damaged goods. If we have lost another person's possessions or if a third party steals them from us, we are obliged to match what was lost in kind or in money. If we have assisted in a theft or in some way benefited from a theft, we must make appropriate restitution.

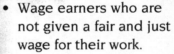

FAITH CONNECTION

Choose one of these four issues: stealing, vandalism, cheating, or discrimination. Work with a partner to design a positive strategy for dealing with the issue in your school. Outline the main points of your strategy in this space.

_____

_____

_____

Saint Francis Preaching to the Birds.
Benazzo Gozzoli (1420–1497), Florentine painter.

Saint Francis of Assisi

The Seventh Commandment guides us to act justly. We are to fulfill our responsibility to be faithful stewards of creation. Saint Francis of Assisi clearly saw that all creation belongs to God. He considered everything a gift from God. He spent his whole life announcing this message to the world.

God gave Francis Bernardone (1181–1226), the son of a wealthy cloth merchant, a special gift. Francis came to know beyond any doubt that he was a creature. God alone is the Creator. Everything, the smallest piece of creation, is a gift from God the Father to all his children.

In his youth Francis was known to use his wealth to entertain his friends. In the year 1202, when Francis was taken prisoner while fighting in a conflict with Perugia, a town not far from Assisi, he began to change. He gave up his extravagant living. To the amazement and ridicule of his friends, he began to live in poverty.

One day while he was at prayer, Francis was inspired to repair a church near Assisi. Francis returned home, took cloth from his father's shop, and sold it to raise money for materials to rebuild the church.

When his father demanded the return of the cloth, Francis returned everything—even the clothes he was wearing—to his father. Francis then put on the simple robe that poor people of his day wore. It is the same type of robe followers of Francis wear today.

The robe of Francis is a sign of his belief that all creation is a sign of God's love for us. This belief of Saint Francis of Assisi is a guide for us to live as faithful stewards of creation. We are to honor and respect all creation out of our honor and respect for God. Pope John Paul II named Saint Francis of Assisi the patron of ecologists in 1979.

How can you follow the example of Saint Francis by being a good steward of all creation?

WHAT DIFFERENCE
Does Faith Make in My Life?

Mixed Media Messages

The Sixth and Ninth Commandments call us to respect our bodies by living chaste lives and to respect the dignity of others. The Seventh Commandment calls us to live in mercy and justice. We are to respect the property of others, and to be good stewards of the environment. Many mixed and false messages in the media tempt us away from faithfully living these commandments.

Do you believe that you are strongly influenced by the media? Does society encourage you to live a good Christian life? Does it sometimes make it more difficult for you to live the Gospel?

Here are a few media messages that you probably see or hear quite often. If you strongly agree, circle SA, strongly agree; A, agree; D, disagree; or SD, strongly disagree. Give reasons for your choices.

- Looking young and handsome or glamorous is the most important thing.

    SA   A   D   SD

- Wealth is the sign of a successful and happy life.

    SA   A   D   SD

- Buy a certain brand of clothing and your peers will accept you.

    SA   A   D   SD

- Violence is not just OK; it is the best way to handle things.

    SA   A   D   SD

- Society says the same thing that Jesus says about love and commitment.

    SA   A   D   SD

- Self-satisfaction and pleasure are the ultimate goals, no matter who else gets hurt.

    SA   A   D   SD

- The way women are pictured and treated in the media affirms their dignity and encourages respect.

    SA   A   D   SD

Be a Truth Seeker

Advertisements and certain messages in the media will always try to convince you that they are telling you the truth and that they always have your best interests at heart. Do you believe this? Start to evaluate the messages you hear. Determine what they are really saying, or selling. When you view a movie, a music video, or a TV show, think about the real message you receive. Are these the values that are important to you? Are these messages the same messages Jesus is encouraging you to listen to and follow? Seek the truth in the media and try not to allow it to change or influence your values and beliefs as a follower of Jesus.

Faith Decision

- In a small group discuss your favorite TV show or movie or music DVD or video and explain the values it portrays.
- Describe how those values respect or reject:

  The Sixth Commandment

  _____

  The Seventh Commandment

  _____

  The Ninth Commandment

  _____

  This week I will determine if media messages encourage me to follow the Sixth, Seventh, and Ninth Commandments, and then I will choose to

  _____
  _____
  _____
  _____
  _____ .

PRAY and REVIEW

Canticle of Brother Sun

Be praised,
my Lord,
with all your
creatures,
especially
Brother Sun!

Be praised,
my Lord,
for Sister Moon
and Stars!
They are bright
and lovely
and fair.

Be praised,
my Lord,
for Brother Wind,
and for Air
and Weather,
cloudy and clear.

Be praised,
my Lord,
for our Sister,
Mother Earth,
who feeds us, and
produces fruits,
colorful flowers,
and leaves.

SAINT FRANCIS OF ASSISI

FAITH VOCABULARY

Define each of these terms:

1. chastity   2. stewardship
3. reparation

MAIN IDEAS

Choose either (a) or (b) from each set of items.
Write a brief paragraph to answer each of
your choices.

1. (a) Discuss ways you can respect and
       honor your gift of sexuality.
   (b) Explain the principles that help you
       live a chaste life.
2. (a) Explain how stealing is an act of
       disrespect.
   (b) Explain what it means to care for
       God's creation.

CRITICAL THINKING

Using what you have learned in this chapter,
briefly explain this statement:
   Reason says that destroying clean air is
   impractical; faith says it dishonors God.

FAMILY DISCUSSION

How do we as a family show our respect
for others?

For more ideas on ways
your family can live your
faith, visit the "Faith First
for Families" page at
www.FaithFirst.com. Also
check out the Teen Center
and read the interactive
story.

The Eighth and Tenth Commandments

11

FAITH FOCUS

How does the Eighth Commandment guide us in living as people of truth?

FAITH VOCABULARY

lying	covet
avarice	greed
envy	

What are some of the challenges you have faced to be honest and generous?

An often-told true story concerns an eleven-year-old contestant from South Carolina who made it to the fourth round of a national spelling contest in Washington, D.C. The contestant was to spell the word *avowal.* When the contestant did so, the judges were not able to agree on whether an "a" or an "e" was used for the second-to-last letter. Finally, the chief judge asked, "How did you spell the word?" "I misspelled the word," the contestant admitted, and graciously left the stage. The Eighth and Tenth Commandments guide us to live lives of honesty and generosity.

Describe how the above story portrays a person living the Ten Commandments.

LORD . . . [g]uide me in your truth and teach me.
PSALM 25:4, 5

Living Truthful Lives

The Eighth Commandment

You shall not bear false witness against your neighbor. EXODUS 20:16

God is Truth and he is always faithful to his word. This is the heart of his covenant with his people. With King David, we praise God, saying:

"Lord GOD, you are God and your words are truth."
2 SAMUEL 7:28

The Eighth Commandment teaches that we are to be people of our word. We are to be people of Truth in whose image we have been created. We are to respect the rights of people to know the truth.

We are to say what we mean. We are not to deliberately deceive other people by saying one thing and meaning another (duplicity). We are not to disguise our true feelings (dissimulation). We are not to pretend to be what we are not or pretend to believe in something we really do not believe in (hypocrisy). The gift of freedom that God has given us does not include, as some wrongly believe, the right to do or say anything.

This commandment also sets the standard for the media. The media—television, the press, the Internet—need to seek out and honestly report only what is truthful.

Bearing False Witness

Telling the truth requires practice. So does telling lies, or bearing false witness. **Lying** is intentionally deceiving another person by deliberately saying what is false. Given enough time and practice, we can become experienced liars. There are several ways that we can bend, twist, and destroy the truth.

- **Perjury.** Perjury is lying under oath.

- **Harming a person's reputation and honor.** Everyone is due an honorable reputation. Rash judgment, detraction, and calumny all injure the reputation and good name of other people.

    Rash judgment occurs when we rush to judge another person's moral standing without sufficient reasons or evidence.

People bear false witness against the Jewish people when they state that all Jewish people, including Jewish people today, are guilty of the crimes committed during Christ's Passion. This is a form of anti-Semitism, which the Church condemns.

Keeping a Confidence

There are situations that demand that we remain silent and not share what we know to be true. We are not obligated to reveal the truth to someone who does not have a right to know it. In fact, in some situations we might even have an obligation not to disclose the truth we know. For example, the sacramental seal of confession can never be broken. The secrecy and confidentiality of conversations between lawyers and their clients are protected by civil law. The fact is that the good and safety of other people, the common good, and the respect for privacy may be sufficient reasons for remaining silent and not sharing what we know to be true.

Detraction is the unjust revealing to a third party of someone else's faults or failings. Gossip can lead to detraction. Calumny is the making of untrue remarks that leads to doubting or questioning another person's reputation or honor.

- **Boasting.** Some people try to earn recognition with their "mouth." They are boasters. Boasters are the people who unnecessarily inflate their accomplishments and abilities.

Telling the truth is vital to our relationships with people. Telling lies tears down trust and separates people from one another. So important is telling the truth that justice demands we repair the damage or harm caused by our acts against the truth.

FAITH CONNECTION

Work with a partner. Describe a situation in which it is difficult and embarrassing to tell the truth. Role-play a solution that portrays what a faithful follower of Jesus would do.

Situation: _____

_____

_____

_____

_____

_____

_____

The Tenth Commandment

You shall not covet your neighbor's goods.

BASED ON EXODUS 20:17

While teaching about the kingdom of heaven, Jesus told his disciples:

"[W]here your treasure is, there also will your heart be." MATTHEW 6:21

The Tenth Commandment, in many ways, guides us in keeping our heart in the right place.

When we **covet** another person's goods, we wrongfully treasure that person's possessions, abilities, talents, friends, achievements, and so on. We crave or lust after the blessings of others. Covetousness is one of the seven capital sins, or sins that are at the root of other sins. The Church has named seven capital sins. They are pride, avarice (covetousness), envy, wrath (anger), lust, gluttony, and sloth.

Coveting what belongs to others can lead to theft, robbery, fraud, and even murder. Read any murder news story and you will probably find some form of coveting going on.

When we desire those possessions out of avarice, greed, or envy, we violate the Tenth Commandment.

Avarice. **Avarice** is one of the seven capital sins. It is an excessive passion for wealth and the power often connected with wealth. It makes a god out of possessions. Think of it this way: It turns a person's heart into a cold, steel bank vault. Avaricious people never seem to have enough. If you analyze the news, you will see how the lives of avaricious people are marked by fraud, theft, and other criminal behaviors.

Desiring to have what another person has is not always wrong. Sometimes desiring the achievements and possessions of other people can motivate us to use the gifts and talents with which God has blessed us. It can motivate us to work harder for good grades, a better job, a place on the starting lineup, and so on.

Our possessions, abilities, and talents—all our blessings—are gifts from God. They are signs of the generosity and love of God for all people. When we honor and respect the blessings of others and seek and obtain our possessions in a just and fair way, our heart is in the right place. We honor and bless God who is the source of all blessings.

Greed. **Greed** is the unchecked desire to have more and more things. For some people, greed becomes a compulsion to have the best or the latest or the trendiest things they can find. No one likes a greedy person.

Envy. Greed is frequently caused by the capital sin of **envy**. Envy blinds us to the truth that all blessings come from God. Envious people are saddened that other people have something they do not have. Envy can lead to hatred of neighbors, telling lies about them, harming their reputations, and even rejoicing at their misfortune. Humility, goodwill, and trust in divine Providence help us see the goodness of our own lives and overcome the temptation of envy (see Matthew 4:7–10, 6:25–34).

Describe characters from books or movies who violate the Tenth Commandment. Give examples and describe the consequences of their actions.

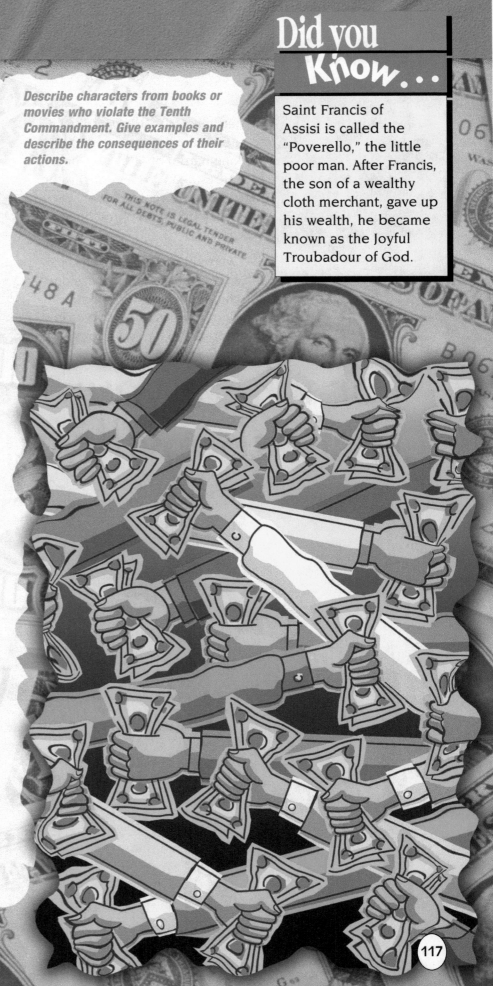

Living the Gospel

In Matthew 6:19–21 Jesus tells us to keep our priorities straight. By working harder at filling our hearts with treasures (possessions) rather than with the Creator, we are setting ourselves up for a spiritual heart attack.

If we want our life with God to thrive, we cannot let possessions attach themselves to us, slow us down, or drag us down and stop us in our tracks. We need to develop the virtue of detachment, as Saint Francis of Assisi did. We need to detach ourselves from our possessions so we can successfully complete our journey to the kingdom of heaven.

Detached people see all material blessings for what they are. They are glimpses of the true happiness God has created us to have. People are truly wealthy who praise and credit God for their blessings and generously share those blessings with others.

For where your treasure is, there also will your heart be.
Matthew 6:21

FAITH CONNECTION

Look up these three Scripture passages. Choose one and describe how it can guide a follower of Christ to live the Gospel.

Matthew 6:24 • Mark 12:41–44 • Luke 6:20

_____

_____

_____

_____

Josephine (1869–1947) was seized in 1875 by slave traders in her home village and given the name Bakhita, "lucky one," by the person to whom she was sold into slavery. Six years later Josephine came to the attention of the Italian vice-consul in Khartoum. He stepped forward, brought Josephine into his family, and freed her from slavery. Josephine returned to Italy with the vice-consul.

Josephine was baptized in 1890. In 1896 she joined the Canosians, a religious community founded by Maddalena of Canossa in Italy. Josephine dedicated her life to serving people in need. Josephine's life journey is a reminder of the evil of slavery and the power of the Gospel to transform a person's life. On October 1, 2000, Pope John Paul II declared Josephine Bakhita to be a saint of the Church. She is the first African to be canonized since the early centuries of the Church, and the first person from Sudan ever to be canonized.

Saint Josephine Bakhita

People of truth recognize that their blessings and the blessings of other people come from God. They recognize that true happiness comes from their life as sons and daughters of God. Standing up for the truth of the Gospel may put us at odds with what people falsely have come to believe is the truth. Josephine Bakhita found herself in that position.

Name a situation you have faced that went against the truth of the Gospel. Did you speak out? Why or why not?

Saint Josephine Bakhita, born in Olgossa, a village in Dafur, Sudan (Africa)

WHAT DIFFERENCE
Does Faith Make in My Life?

Peer Pressure

In this chapter you learned how the Eighth and Tenth Commandments guide you in living as people of truth who respect other people and their possessions. These two commandments call us to respect others but not to be pressured or negatively influenced by them.

Peer pressure has influenced children and adults for centuries. We usually think of peer pressure as negative, but in fact it can also be positive. In the negative sense, peer pressure means giving in to what your peers are telling you to do even though you know it is not the right decision to make. It is a pressure to go along with the crowd, even if it means going against your own better judgment. In the positive sense, peer pressure can influence you to do what is right and make good choices at times when you need extra courage or strength.

Negative Forms of Peer Pressure

Here are a few examples of negative peer pressure.

▼ **Collusion** is a conspiracy or an agreement that a few people make for a negative or nasty purpose. Usually, it means they make up a lie or a rumor and try to convince others to go along with it. For example, sometimes

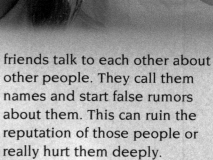

friends talk to each other about other people. They call them names and start false rumors about them. This can ruin the reputation of those people or really hurt them deeply.

▼ **Bullies** try to boss, threaten, and control others. Bullies pick on or make fun of other students who may then become outcasts of the class and the brunt of cruel jokes.

▼ **Group peer pressure** occurs when the crowd decides to do something you know is wrong or something you would never choose to do on your own. It is difficult to resist one person's influence. It is even harder to go against an entire group.

Powerful Positive Peer Pressure

How can you stand up for what you believe? How can you really be a powerful positive influence for your friends and allow them to be the same for you? Here are a few suggestions.

▲ **Instinct.** Trust your own instincts. Probably your so-called friends won't have your best interests at heart anyway if they are convincing you to do what is wrong. You know right from wrong. Pray for the grace and strength to stand up for your beliefs.

▲ **Respect.** Create a healthy environment among your friends. Reach out to others too. Treat each other with respect. Join together to listen, support, and encourage one another. Be models of acceptance to the rest of your school.

▲ **Support.** Your group can be a wonderful source of compassion, sympathy, affection, and understanding. Your group can be a safe place to help your friends discover themselves and learn about each other. It can provide a powerful, positive place for peer emotional support.

Faith Decision

In small groups discuss how your group could work to be a positive force among your peers. Respond to these questions to get your discussion started:

• How would observing the Eighth Commandment help you achieve this goal?

_____

• How would observing the Tenth Commandment help you achieve this goal?

_____

• How difficult do you think achieving this goal might be? What obstacles might you have to overcome?

_____

This week I will ask the Holy Spirit to give me the good judgment and courage to be a postive influence among my peers by

_____

_____.

PRAY and REVIEW

Prayer for Peace

Leader:
Lord Jesus Christ, you
are the Prince of Peace.

All:
Grant us peace.

Leader:
Make all men and
women witnesses of brotherly love.

All:
Grant us peace.

Leader:
Banish from our hearts
whatever might endanger peace.

All:
Grant us peace.

Leader:
Enlighten our rulers
that they may defend the great gift
of peace.

All:
Grant us peace.

Leader:
May all peoples on the
earth become as brothers
and sisters.

All:
**May longed-for peace
blossom forth and reign always
over us all. Amen.**

BASED ON A PRAYER FOR PEACE
BY POPE JOHN PAUL II

FAITH VOCABULARY

Define each of these terms:

1. lying
2. covet
3. avarice
4. greed
5. envy

MAIN IDEAS

Choose either (a) or (b) from each set of items. Write a brief paragraph to answer each of your choices.

1. (a) Describe how the Eighth Commandment guides us to live as followers of Christ.
   (b) Explain what "bearing false witness" means.

2. (a) Describe how the Tenth Commandment guides us in living as followers of Christ.
   (b) Explain what "coveting" means.

CRITICAL THINKING

Using what you have learned in this chapter, briefly explain this verse from the Gospel according to Matthew:
"For where your treasure is, there also will your heart be."   MATTHEW 6:21

FAMILY DISCUSSION

What one thing does our family most seek? Why is that?

For more ideas on ways your family can live your faith, visit the "Faith First for Families" page at **www.FaithFirst.com**. Also check out the extra activity for this chapter on the Teen Center.

The Lord's Prayer

12

When do you plan what you will do?

Architects draw up plans and blueprints that detail the structures they intend to build. Jesus gave us a plan and a blueprint for building our life when he taught his disciples the Lord's Prayer.

Why do you think Christians pray the Lord's Prayer every day?

For the kingdom, the power and the glory are yours now and for ever.

FROM *ROMAN MISSAL*, LORD'S PRAYER, DOXOLOGY

Summary of the Gospel

The **Lord's Prayer,** or the Our Father, is in some ways a blueprint for living the Gospel and making it come alive in our lives. It is the prayer that Jesus, the architect of the Gospel, gave to his followers. The Christian writer Tertullian (ca. 160–225) described the Lord's Prayer as "the summary of the whole Gospel." Not many years later Saint Augustine of Hippo (354–430) wrote:

> Run through all the words of the holy prayers [in Scripture] and I do not think that you will find anything in them that is not contained and included in the Lord's Prayer.

Jesus, the master and model of prayer for Christians, taught us to pray the Our Father. Flowing from Jesus' heart, this prayer expresses the intimacy between Jesus and his Father. By giving us this prayer, Jesus invites us to share in that intimacy.

Christ Hugging People. Nip Rogers, contemporary artist/graphic illustrator.

The Sermon on the Mount is a collection of Jesus' teachings. It states the blueprint for Christian living. Beginning with the Beatitudes, it contains the basic values and attitudes that give shape to the lives of all Christians. The Gospel according to Luke has a section similar to Matthew's Sermon on the Mount. It is found in Luke 6:20–49.

The Lord's Prayer

The Lord's Prayer is part of the Sermon on the Mount in Matthew's account of the Gospel. Jesus said:

> "This is how you are to pray:
> Our Father in heaven,
>   hallowed be your name,
>   your kingdom come,
>   your will be done,
>   on earth as in heaven.
> Give us today our daily bread;
> and forgive us our debts,
>   as we forgive our debtors;
> and do not subject us to the
>   final test,
> but deliver us from the
>   evil one." MATTHEW 6:9–13

Jesus concluded:

> "If you forgive others their transgressions, your heavenly Father will forgive you. But if you do not forgive others, neither will your Father forgive your transgressions." MATTHEW 6:14–15

On the surface, the words of the Lord's Prayer are simple enough. But there is sufficient meat here to provide us food for meditation for a lifetime. The first half of the Lord's Prayer describes our belief in God and his plan for us. The second half presents our needs to God.

FAITH CONNECTION

In small groups describe gestures you can include in praying the Our Father.

Our Father _____

hallowed be thy name _____

Thy kingdom come _____

Thy will . . . in heaven _____

Give us our daily bread _____

forgive us . . . _____

as we forgive . . . _____

lead us not into temptation _____

deliver us from evil _____

Our Father in Heaven

The first words we speak in a conversation are always important. Our opening words set the tone for the remainder of the conversation.

The very first words of address in the Lord's Prayer set the tone of our meeting with God in prayer. We say, "Our Father in heaven." God is our loving, caring, faithful Father. His love for us has no limits. He is the One who always walks by our side.

God is the Father of everyone. He is the God of heaven and earth, the Almighty One, the Creator. He has entered into a covenant of friendship with his people.

Explain the importance of Jesus beginning the prayer with the words "Our Father in heaven."

Hallowed Be Thy Name

After addressing God as Father, we pray seven petitions. The first three petitions focus on God and acknowledge that God is the center of our lives. The final four petitions acknowledge our dependence on God for our every need and our very life.

In the first petition, we acknowledge the goodness and holiness of God. God is so good that we describe his very name as holy. God created us to share in his holiness. We are to live holy lives. In Jesus' final prayer for his disciples, he prayed:

"Holy Father, keep them in your name that you have given me, so that they may be one just as we are." JOHN 17:11

With the birth of the Church, we experience the overwhelming goodness and holiness of God in the celebration of the sacraments, in prayer, and in the example and witness of believers as they live their faith.

"I bore you up on eagle wings and brought you here to myself."

Exodus 19:4

Thy Kingdom Come

At the heart of Jesus' preaching is the announcement of the coming of the kingdom of God (see Matthew 3:2, Mark 1:15). In the second petition, we profess our belief that God has created all people to live in communion with him and with one another and with all creation not only on earth but forever in heaven. We believe and hope that kingdom will come when Christ comes again in glory.

Thy Will Be Done on Earth as It Is in Heaven

God's will is that his loving plan of creation and salvation be brought to completion. In the third petition, we affirm not only that God loves us, cares for us, and has a plan for us; we also affirm that we will live in such a way to work at bringing about God's will—God's plan, God's kingdom.

God has not left us alone to know and do his will. The Son of God became human to help us know what God's will is for us. The Father and the Son have sent the Holy Spirit to guide us in discovering

and understanding God's will. The grace of God strengthens us to make God's will the foundation of our lives.

What might you do to better prepare for the coming of the kingdom of God?

Give Us This Day Our Daily Bread

Jesus taught us:

"What father among you would hand his son a snake when he asks for a fish? . . . [H]ow much more will the Father in heaven give?"   LUKE 11:11, 13

It is with trust and confidence that we place our spiritual and material needs ("our daily bread") before God. We not only talk to God about ourselves; we also pray with and for one another. We resolve to look for and work for solutions to the human problems that stand in the way of the coming of the kingdom of God.

The Gospel describes how Jesus was tempted by the devil at the beginning of his ministry. You can read about the temptation of Jesus in Matthew 4:1–11.

Forgive Us Our Trespasses as We Forgive Those Who Trespass Against Us

In this petition we acknowledge that we sometimes turn our hearts away from God's love. We sin. Recalling the words Jesus spoke after he taught the disciples the Our Father helps us understand the meaning of what we are saying. Jesus said:

"If you forgive others their transgressions, your heavenly Father will forgive you. But if you do not forgive others, neither will your Father forgive your transgressions." MATTHEW 6:14–15

It is a simple fact that our forgiveness must have no limits (see Matthew 18:2–22).

Lead Us Not into Temptation

Temptation is all that moves us away from living holy lives. In this petition we ask for the guidance of the Holy Spirit to see the truth in every situation and to recognize evil for the lie that it is.

Deliver Us from Evil

At the Last Supper Jesus said:

"I do not ask that you take them out of the world but that you keep them from the evil one." JOHN 17:15

It is the "evil one," Satan, from whom Jesus asks us to be delivered. He is the one whom Jesus calls "a murderer from the beginning . . . a liar and the father of lies" (John 8:44).

Filled with the Holy Spirit we confidently share our deepest hopes with God our Father. We pray and hope that we will share now and forever in the victory of Jesus over evil and death in all its forms.

FAITH CONNECTION

In your journal or in this space share why the Lord's Prayer is a prayer of trust and hope.

OUR CHURCH
MAKES A DIFFERENCE

Catholic Relief Services

When the crowd asked Jesus to teach them to pray, he taught them the Our Father, or Lord's Prayer. In teaching them this prayer, Jesus not only taught them how to pray but also gave them a blueprint for living the Gospel. In the Our Father, we pray, "Give us this day our daily bread." We pray for our own material and spiritual needs as well as the needs of others. The Catholic Relief Services puts those words of the Our Father into action.

Newspaper headlines regularly tell of sufferings and needs of people around the globe. "Earthquake Shakes Mexico." "War Ravages the Middle East." "Famine Spreads in Africa." "Hurricanes Pound Puerto Rico." These headlines are accompanied by vivid pictures that bring the sufferings and needs of people into our living rooms. They also bring Catholic Relief Services into action.

Catholic Relief Services was founded in 1943 by the Catholic bishops in the United States to respond to the victims of disaster outside the United States. The ministry of Catholic Relief Services is the Gospel being lived. It bases its ministry on the Scriptures and the social teachings of the Catholic Church. In the Gospel Jesus Christ calls all people to work to alleviate human suffering. He clearly tells us that when we feed or clothe or give drink to someone in need, we are doing these things for him.

The ministry of Catholic Relief Services proclaims and lives the Gospel in more than eighty countries around the world. Every time Catholic Relief Services workers reach out to others, they proclaim the moral responsibility of all people toward all people. They teach us that God is the Father of all people.

How can you live the petition "Give us this day our daily bread," which we pray in the Our Father?

WHAT DIFFERENCE
Does Faith Make in My Life?

Consumerism

In the Our Father we pray, "Give us this day our daily bread." We ask God to give us what we need to live caring, happy lives. It is easy sometimes to confuse what we really need with what we want. Much of that confusion stems from what we refer to as consumerism. Put yourself in this familiar scene.

As the music grows louder and louder, you are told you cannot possibly live without eating this certain food. The super action and special effects lure you to stay glued to the TV. You are labeled a loser or not cool unless you own these brand-name shoes or jeans. You absolutely cannot function unless you have this particular CD, DVD, or the latest big-screen TV. You are constantly bombarded on the radio, TV, and billboards by thousands of advertisements that promise to enhance your life.

Consumerism can be defined as the strong promotion of products that interest potential customers to buy certain things that will satisfy their wishes and wants.

The youth of today have been labeled "consumers in training." According to marketers in big businesses, young people have tremendous spending power and great economic clout. Companies want to convince you while you are young and impressionable to buy their products and be loyal to their name brand. Advertisements target teenagers to persuade them to buy a particular, usually more expensive, item and convince them that they really need it and must have it.

The Pope's Challenge

Blessed Pope John Paul II challenged the youth of today to fight against consumerism, to stop instant self-gratification, and to grow in the gift of service and compassion. The challenge is not to be tricked or fooled by some half-truths or misleading suggestions that encourage you to buy things you do not even need. The virtue of temperance reminds you to understand the difference between needs and wants. Yes, you like to own a lot of possessions—things that give you pleasure and make you feel good—but these are usually "wants." How can you resist the temptation to buy or own the latest and greatest "thing" and maintain control and balance over your choices? Remember that you are in charge of your possessions; you are not a slave to them.

What Can You Do?

Here are some skills to help you answer the pope's challenge to avoid consumerism.

◆ **Be an informed customer.** Look at the facts about a product. If you don't need it, don't let someone convince you to buy it.

◆ **Respect yourself.** Your self-esteem does not depend on brand-name possessions.

◆ **Analyze the advertisement.** Talk about it with your family and friends. What hook or gimmick is the company using to convince you to buy their product?

◆ **Be a comparison shopper.** Evaluate the product for quality, price, and actual need.

◆ **Be generous and compassionate.** Hold back on your desire for instant gratification and set aside that money to donate to a good cause. Create a handmade gift or card to give to someone you love or to someone who is lonely.

Faith Decision

In small groups in class and with family members at home talk about some of the advertisements that influence you the most. Discuss these and similar questions.

- How does each advertisement try to convince you that this product is something you really need?

- How can you support one another in recognizing the difference between what you really need and what you want?

- How can practicing the virtue of temperance help you grow in love and service of others?

This week I will accept Pope John Paul II's challenge to fight consumerism and instant gratification by

_____

_____

_____

_____

_____

_____ .

PRAY and REVIEW

Prayer for Reconciliation

Leader:

(A)lmighty and eternal God . . .
you constantly offer pardon
and call on sinners
to trust in your forgiveness alone.

All:

We turn our hearts to you.

Group 1:

Never did you turn away from us,
. . . though time and time again
    we have broken your covenant, . . .

All:

We turn our hearts to you.

Group 2:

(Y)ou have bound the human family
    to yourself
through Jesus your Son,
    our Redeemer,
with a new bond of love so tight
    that it can never be undone.

All:

We turn our hearts to you.

Group 3:

Even now you set before
    your people
a time of grace and reconciliation, . . .

All:

We turn our hearts to you.

FROM EUCHARISTIC PRAYER FOR RECONCILIATION I

FAITH VOCABULARY

Use each of these terms correctly in a sentence.

1. Lord's Prayer   2. temptation

MAIN IDEAS

Choose either (a) or (b) from each set of items. Write a brief paragraph to answer each of your choices.

1. (a) Describe the Lord's Prayer as a blueprint for living the Gospel.
   (b) Explain how the Lord's Prayer provides us with "food for meditation for a lifetime."
2. (a) Describe the focus of the first three petitions of the Lord's Prayer.
   (b) Describe the focus of the final four petitions of the Lord's Prayer.

CRITICAL THINKING

Using what you have learned in this chapter, explain the meaning of this statement:
"You cannot call the God of all kindness your Father if you preserve a cruel and inhuman heart."   SAINT JOHN CHYRSOSTOM

FAMILY DISCUSSION

Since we ask God to "give us this day our daily bread," we too must do the same for one another. What is the "daily bread" we need to share with one another?

For more ideas on ways your family can live your faith, visit the "Faith First for Families" page at **www.FaithFirst.com**. Also check out the latest games on the Teen Center.

UNIT TWO
REVIEWREVIEW

A. The Best Response

Read each statement and circle the best answer.

1. What do we call those things that people can choose to take the place of God in their lives?
   - A. idols
   - B. false gods
   - C. money or power
   - D. all of the above

2. What does it mean to remember to keep holy the Lord's Day?
   - A. honoring God only on the third day of every week
   - B. keeping Sunday as a day set aside to worship God and re-create our relationship with him
   - C. preserving one day a week to sleep
   - D. remembering to go to church once a month

3. Which of the following is an example of keeping the Fifth Commandment?
   - A. abortion
   - B. respecting life
   - C. euthanasia
   - D. taking illegal drugs

4. Placing an intimate sexual relationship only within a lifelong marriage is in accordance with which of the Ten Commandments?
   - A. the Fifth Commandment
   - B. the Sixth Commandment
   - C. the Tenth Commandment
   - D. none of the above

5. The Seventh Commandment, which tells us to fulfill responsibly the call to manage and care for all God's creation, relates to _____.
   - A. stewardship
   - B. temperance
   - C. control
   - D. fortitude

B. Matching Words and Phrases

Match the terms in column A with the descriptions in column B.

Column A	Column B
_____ 1. temptation	a. principles or laws
_____ 2. direct abortion	b. intentional killing of an unborn child
_____ 3. greed	c. killing of a person suffering from a long-term illness
_____ 4. reparation	d. to pay for misdeeds
_____ 5. lying	e. intentionally deceiving another person
_____ 6. avarice	f. excessive passion for wealth and power
_____ 7. euthanasia	g. unchecked desire to have more and more
_____ 8. precepts	h. a lure to do evil or sin
_____ 9. perjury	i. lying under oath
_____ 10. boasting	j. inflating one's accomplishments

C. What I Have Learned

Using what you learned in this unit, write a two-sentence reflection about each of the following statements.

God is the Author of human life.

_____

_____

The Our Father is the blueprint for living the Gospel.

_____

_____

D. A Scripture Story

On a separate sheet of paper do the following:

Recall the story of Martha and Mary. Which of these women is more like you? What could you do to develop some of the qualities you are lacking? Do you need to do more to develop a life of prayer?

Catholic Prayers and Practices

Sign of the Cross

In the name of the Father,
and of the Son,
and of the Holy Spirit. Amen.

Signum Crucis

In nómine Patris,
et Fílii,
et Spíritus Sancti. Amen.

Glory Be

Glory be to the Father
and to the Son
and to the Holy Spirit,
as it was in the beginning is now,
and ever shall be
world without end. Amen.

Gloria Patri

Glória Patri
et Fílio
et Spirítui Sancto.
Sicut erat in princípio,
et nunc et semper
et in sæcula sæculórum. Amen.

Lord's Prayer

Our Father, who art in heaven,
hallowed be thy name;
thy kingdom come,
thy will be done on earth
    as it is in heaven.
Give us this day our daily bread,
and forgive us our trespasses,
as we forgive those who trespass
    against us;
and lead us not into temptation,
but deliver us from evil. Amen.

Pater Noster

Pater noster, qui es in cælis:
sanctificétur nomen tuum;
advéniat regnum tuum;
fiat volúntas tua, sicut in cælo, et in terra.
Panem nostrum cotidiánum
    da nobis hódie;
et dimítte nobis débita nostra,
sicut et nos dimíttimus debitóribus nostris;
et ne nos indúcas in tentatiónem;
sed líbera nos a malo. Amen.

Hail Mary

Hail, Mary, full of grace,
the Lord is with thee.
Blessed art thou among women,
and blessed is the fruit
    of thy womb, Jesus.
Holy Mary, Mother of God,
pray for us sinners,
now and at the hour of our death.
Amen.

Ave, Maria

Ave, María, grátia plena,
Dóminus tecum.
Benedícta tu in muliéribus,
et benedíctus fructus ventris tui, Jesus.
Sancta María, Mater Dei,
ora pro nobis peccatóribus,
nunc et in hora mortis nostræ. Amen.

Nicene Creed

I believe in one God,
the Father almighty,
maker of heaven and earth,
of all things visible and invisible.

I believe in one Lord Jesus Christ,
the Only Begotten Son of God,
born of the Father before all ages.
God from God, Light from Light,
true God from true God,
begotten, not made, consubstantial
    with the Father;
through him all things were made.
For us men and for our salvation
he came down from heaven,
and by the Holy Spirit was incarnate
    of the Virgin Mary,
and became man.

For our sake he was crucified under
    Pontius Pilate,
he suffered death and was buried,
and rose again on the third day
in accordance with the Scriptures.
He ascended into heaven
and is seated at the right hand of the Father.
He will come again in glory
to judge the living and the dead
and his kingdom will have no end.

I believe in the Holy Spirit, the Lord,
    the giver of life,
who proceeds from the Father and the Son,
who with the Father and the Son
    is adored and glorified,
who has spoken through the prophets.

I believe in one, holy, catholic and
    apostolic Church.
I confess one Baptism for the forgiveness of sins
and I look forward to the resurrection of the dead
    and the life of the world to come.
Amen.

Apostles' Creed

I believe in God,
the Father almighty,
Creator of heaven and earth,
and in Jesus Christ, his only Son, our Lord,
who was conceived by the Holy Spirit,
born of the Virgin Mary,
suffered under Pontius Pilate,
was crucified, died and was buried;
he descended into hell;
on the third day he rose again from the dead;
he ascended into heaven,
and is seated at the right hand of God
    the Father almighty;
from there he will come to judge the living
    and the dead.

I believe in the Holy Spirit,
the holy catholic Church,
the communion of saints,
the forgiveness of sins,
the resurrection of the body,
and life everlasting. Amen.

Morning Prayer

Dear God,
as I begin this day,
keep me in your love and care.
Help me to live as your child today.
Bless me, my family, and my friends in all we do.
Keep us all close to you. Amen.

Evening Prayer

Dear God,
I thank you for today.
Keep me safe throughout the night.
Thank you for all the good I did today.
I am sorry for what I have chosen to do wrong.
Bless my family and friends. Amen.

Grace before Meals

Bless us, O Lord,
    and these thy gifts,
which we are about to receive
    from thy bounty,
through Christ our Lord. Amen.

Grace after Meals

We give thee thanks, for all thy benefits,
    almighty God,
who lives and reigns forever. Amen.

The Divine Praises

Blessed be God.
Blessed be his holy name.
Blessed be Jesus Christ, true God and true man.
Blessed be the name of Jesus.
Blessed be his most Sacred Heart.
Blessed be his most precious Blood.
Blessed be Jesus in the most holy Sacrament
    of the altar.
Blessed be the Holy Spirit, the Paraclete.
Blessed be the great Mother of God, Mary
    most holy.
Blessed be her holy and Immaculate
    Conception.
Blessed be her glorious Assumption.
Blessed be the name of Mary, Virgin and Mother.
Blessed be Saint Joseph, her most chaste spouse.
Blessed be God in his angels and in his saints.

Prayer to the Holy Spirit

Come, Holy Spirit, fill the hearts
    of your faithful.
And kindle in them the
    fire of your love.
Send forth your Spirit and
    they shall be created.
And you will renew the
    face of the earth.

Act of Faith

My God, I firmly believe that you are one God in
three divine Persons, Father, Son, and Holy
Spirit; I believe that your divine Son became
man and died for our sins, and that he will come
to judge the living and the dead. Amen.

Act of Hope

My God, relying on your infinite goodness and
promises, I hope to obtain pardon of my sins, the
help of your grace, and life everlasting, through
the merits of Jesus Christ, my Lord and
Redeemer. Amen.

Act of Love

My God, I love you above all things, with my
whole heart and soul, because you are all good
and worthy of all my love. I love my neighbor as
myself for the love of you. I forgive all who have
injured me and I ask pardon of all whom I have
injured. Amen.

The Trinity,
stained glass

Magnificat

My soul proclaims the greatness
of the Lord,
my spirit rejoices in God my Savior
for he has looked with favor
on his lowly servant.

From this day all generations
will call me blessed:
the Almighty has done great things
for me,
and holy is his name.

He has mercy on those
who fear him
in every generation.

He has shown the strength
of his arm,
he has scattered the proud
in their conceit.

He has cast down the mighty
from their thrones,
and has lifted up the lowly.

He has filled the hungry
with good things,
and the rich he has sent away empty.

He has come to the help
of his servant Israel
for he has remembered
his promise of mercy,
the promise he made to our fathers,
to Abraham and his children for ever.

BASED ON LUKE 1:46–55
FROM CATHOLIC HOUSEHOLD BLESSINGS AND PRAYERS

Memorare

Remember, O most gracious Virgin Mary,
that never was it known
that anyone who fled to your protection,
implored your help,
or sought your intercession was left unaided.

Inspired by this confidence,
I fly unto you, O Virgin of virgins, my mother;
to you do I come,
before you I stand, sinful and sorrowful.

O Mother of the Word Incarnate,
despise not my petitions,
but in your mercy
hear and answer me.
Amen.

Our Lady
of the
Rosary

Rosary

Catholics pray the Rosary to honor Mary and remember the important events in the life of Jesus and Mary. We begin praying the Rosary by praying the Apostles' Creed, the Lord's Prayer, and three Hail Marys. Each mystery of the Rosary is prayed by praying the Lord's Prayer once, the Hail Mary ten times, and the Glory Be once. When we have finished the last mystery, we pray the Hail, Holy Queen.

Joyful Mysteries

1. The Annunciation
2. The Visitation
3. The Nativity
4. The Presentation in the Temple
5. The Finding of the Child Jesus After Three Days in the Temple

Luminous Mysteries

1. The Baptism at the Jordan
2. The Miracle at Cana
3. The Proclamation of the Kingdom and the Call to Conversion
4. The Transfiguration
5. The Institution of the Eucharist

Sorrowful Mysteries

1. The Agony in the Garden
2. The Scourging at the Pillar
3. The Crowning with Thorns
4. The Carrying of the Cross
5. The Crucifixion and Death

Glorious Mysteries

1. The Resurrection
2. The Ascension
3. The Descent of the Holy Spirit at Pentecost
4. The Assumption of Mary
5. The Coronation of the Blessed Virgin as Queen of Heaven and Earth

Hail, Holy Queen

Hail, holy Queen, Mother of mercy,
Hail, our life, our sweetness,
    and our hope.
To you do we cry, poor banished children of Eve.
To you do we send up our sighs,
mourning and weeping
    in this valley of tears.
Turn then, most gracious advocate,
your eyes of mercy toward us;
and after this our exile
show unto us the blessed fruit
    of your womb, Jesus.
O clement, O loving, O sweet
    Virgin Mary.

Stations of the Cross

1. Jesus is condemned to death.

2. Jesus accepts his cross.

3. Jesus falls the first time.

4. Jesus meets his mother.

5. Simon helps Jesus carry the cross.

6. Veronica wipes the face of Jesus.

7. Jesus falls the second time.

8. Jesus meets the women.

9. Jesus falls the third time.

10. Jesus is stripped of his clothes.

11. Jesus is nailed to the cross.

12. Jesus dies on the cross.

13. Jesus is taken down from the cross.

14. Jesus is buried in the tomb.

Some parishes conclude the Stations by reflecting on the Resurrection of Jesus.

The Great Commandment

"You shall love the Lord,
your God, with all your
heart, with all your soul,
and with all your mind. . . .
You shall love your neighbor as yourself."

MATTHEW 22:37, 39

The Ten Commandments

1. I am the LORD your God: you shall not have strange gods before me.
2. You shall not take the name of the LORD your God in vain.
3. Remember to keep holy the LORD's Day.
4. Honor your father and your mother.
5. You shall not kill.
6. You shall not commit adultery.
7. You shall not steal.
8. You shall not bear false witness against your neighbor.
9. You shall not covet your neighbor's wife.
10. You shall not covet your neighbor's goods.

Precepts of the Church

1. Participate in Mass on Sundays and holy days of obligation and rest from unnecessary work.
2. Confess sins at least once a year.
3. Receive Holy Communion at least during the Easter season.
4. Observe the prescribed days of fasting and abstinence.
5. Provide for the material needs of the Church, according to one's abilities.

The Beatitudes

"Blessed are the poor in spirit,
    for theirs is the kingdom of heaven.
Blessed are they who mourn,
    for they will be comforted.
Blessed are the meek,
    for they will inherit the land.
Blessed are they who hunger
        and thirst for righteousness,
    for they will be satisfied.
Blessed are the merciful,
    for they will be shown mercy.
Blessed are the clean of heart,
    for they will see God.
Blessed are the peacemakers,
    for they will be called children of God.
Blessed are they who are persecuted for the
        sake of righteousness,
    for theirs is the kingdom of heaven.

"Blessed are you when they insult you and persecute you and utter every kind of evil against you [falsely] because of me. Rejoice and be glad, for your reward will be great in heaven."

MATTHEW 5:3–12

The Beatitude Window,
stained glass.
Jerry Sodorff, artist.

Theological Virtues

Faith
Hope
Love

Cardinal, or Moral, Virtues

Prudence
Justice
Fortitude
Temperance

Corporal Works of Mercy

Feed people who are hungry.
Give drink to people who are thirsty.
Clothe people who need clothes.
Visit prisoners.
Shelter people who are homeless.
Visit people who are sick.
Bury people who have died.

Spiritual Works of Mercy

Help people who sin.
Teach people who are ignorant.
Give advice to people who have doubts.
Comfort people who suffer.
Be patient with other people.
Forgive people who hurt you.
Pray for people who are alive and
    for those who have died.

Gifts of the Holy Spirit

Wisdom
Understanding
Right judgment (Counsel)
Courage (Fortitude)
Knowledge
Reverence (Piety)
Wonder and awe (Fear of the Lord)

Fruits of the Holy Spirit

Love
Joy
Peace
Patience
Kindness
Goodness
Generosity
Gentleness
Faithfulness
Modesty
Self-control
Chastity

Faith, Hope, and Charity, stained glass

Basic Principles of the Church's Teaching on Social Justice

The Church's teaching on social justice guides us in living lives of holiness and building a just society. These principles are:

1. All human life is sacred. The basic equality of all people flows from their dignity as human persons and the rights that flow from that dignity.

2. The human person is the principle, the object, and the subject of every social group.

3. The human person has been created by God to belong to and to participate in a family and other social communities.

4. Respect for the rights of people flows from their dignity as persons. Society and all social organizations must promote virtue and protect human life and human rights and guarantee the conditions that promote the exercise of freedom.

5. Political communities and public authority are based on human nature. They belong to an order established by God.

6. All human authority must be used for the common good of society.

7. The common good of society consists of respect for and promotion of the fundamental rights of the human person, the just development of material and spiritual goods of society, and the peace and safety of all people.

8. We need to work to eliminate the sinful inequalities that exist between peoples and for the improvement of the living conditions of people. The needs of the poor and vulnerable have a priority.

9. We are one human and global family. We are to share our spiritual blessings, even more than our material blessings.

Based on the *Catechism of the Catholic Church*

The Seven Sacraments

Jesus gave the Church the seven sacraments. The sacraments are the main liturgical signs of the Church. They make the Paschal Mystery of Jesus, who is always the main celebrant of each sacrament, present to us. They make us sharers in the saving work of Christ and in the life of the Holy Trinity.

Sacraments of Initiation

Baptism
We are joined to Jesus Christ, become members of the Church, receive the gift of the Holy Spirit, and are reborn as God's adopted children. Original and all personal sins are forgiven.

Confirmation
Our Baptism is sealed with the gift of the Holy Spirit.

Eucharist
We receive the Body and Blood of Christ who is truly and really present under the appearances of bread and wine. We share in the one sacrifice of Christ. Sharing in the Eucharist most fully joins us to Christ and to the Church.

Sacraments of Healing

Penance and Reconciliation
We receive God's gift of forgiveness and peace.

Anointing of the Sick
Jesus' work of healing is continued in our lives and strengthens our faith and trust in God when we are seriously ill or dying.

Sacraments at the Service of Communion

Holy Orders
A baptized man is ordained and consecrated to serve the Church as a bishop, priest, or deacon.

Matrimony
A baptized man and a baptized woman are united in a lifelong bond of faithful love. They become a sign of God's love for all people and of Christ's love for the Church.

Baptism   Eucharist   Confirmation   Matrimony

Penance and Reconciliation   Holy Orders   Anointing of the Sick

Celebrating the Mass

The Introductory Rites

The Entrance
Sign of the Cross
  and Greeting
The Penitential Act
The Gloria
The Collect

The Liturgy of the Word

The First Reading
  (Usually from the
  Old Testament)
The Psalm
The Second Reading
  (Usually from New
  Testament Letters)
The Gospel Acclamation
The Gospel
The Homily
The Profession of Faith
Prayer of the Faithful

The Liturgy of the Eucharist

The Preparation of the Gifts
The Prayer over the Offerings
The Eucharistic Prayer
The Communion Rite
  The Lord's Prayer
  The Sign of Peace
  The Fraction
  Communion
The Prayer After Communion

The Concluding Rites

The Greeting
The Blessing
The Dismissal

Celebrating Penance and Reconciliation

Individual Rite of Reconciliation

Greeting

Scripture Reading

Confession of Sins

Act of Contrition

Absolution

Closing Prayer

Communal Rite of Reconciliation

Greeting

Scripture Reading

Homily

Examination of Conscience with Litany of
  Contrition and the Lord's Prayer

Individual Confession and Absolution

Closing Prayer

Act of Contrition

My God,
I am sorry for my sins with all my heart.
In choosing to do wrong
and failing to do good,
I have sinned against you
whom I should love above all things.
I firmly intend, with your help,
to do penance,
to sin no more,
and to avoid whatever leads me to sin.
Our Savior Jesus Christ
suffered and died for us.
In his name, my God, have mercy.

The Books of the Bible

The Old Testament

Law (Torah) or Pentateuch

Genesis	(Gn)
Exodus	(Ex)
Leviticus	(Lv)
Numbers	(Nm)
Deuteronomy	(Dt)

Historical Books

Joshua	(Jos)
Judges	(Jgs)
Ruth	(Ru)
First Book of Samuel	(1 Sm)
Second Book of Samuel	(2 Sm)
First Book of Kings	(1 Kgs)
Second Book of Kings	(2 Kgs)
First Book of Chronicles	(1 Chr)
Second Book of Chronicles	(2 Chr)
Ezra	(Ezr)
Nehemiah	(Neh)
Tobit	(Tb)
Judith	(Jdt)
Esther	(Est)
First Book of Maccabees	(1 Mc)
Second Book of Maccabees	(2 Mc)

The Poetry and Wisdom Books

Job	(Jb)
Psalms	(Ps)
Proverbs	(Prv)
Ecclesiastes	(Eccl)
Song of Songs	(Sg)
Wisdom	(Wis)
Sirach/Ecclesiasticus	(Sir)

Prophets

Isaiah	(Is)
Jeremiah	(Jer)
Lamentations	(Lam)
Baruch	(Bar)
Ezekiel	(Ez)
Daniel	(Dn)
Hosea	(Hos)
Joel	(Jl)
Amos	(Am)
Obadiah	(Ob)
Jonah	(Jon)
Micah	(Mi)
Nahum	(Na)
Habakkuk	(Hb)
Zephaniah	(Zep)
Haggai	(Hg)
Zechariah	(Zec)
Malachi	(Mal)

The New Testament

The Gospels

Matthew	(Mt)
Mark	(Mk)
Luke	(Lk)
John	(Jn)

Early Church

Acts of the Apostles	(Acts)

Letters of Paul and Other Letters

Romans	(Rom)
First Letter to the Corinthians	(1 Cor)
Second Letter to the Corinthians	(2 Cor)
Galatians	(Gal)
Ephesians	(Eph)
Philippians	(Phil)
Colossians	(Col)
First Letter to the Thessalonians	(1 Thes)
Second Letter to the Thessalonians	(2 Thes)
First Letter to Timothy	(1 Tm)
Second Letter to Timothy	(2 Tm)
Titus	(Ti)
Philemon	(Phlm)
Hebrews	(Heb)
James	(Jas)
First Letter of Peter	(1 Pt)
Second Letter of Peter	(2 Pt)
First Letter of John	(1 Jn)
Second Letter of John	(2 Jn)
Third Letter of John	(3 Jn)
Jude	(Jude)

Revelation

Revelation	(Rv)

A

abortion (direct)
The intentional killing of a child conceived but not yet born; that is, an unborn child who is still living in the mother's womb.

actual grace
God-given divine help empowering us to live as his adopted daughters and sons.

Anointing of the Sick
A Sacrament of Healing. This sacrament confers the grace of strengthening our faith and trust in God when we are seriously ill, weakened by old age, or dying.

Ark of the Covenant
An elaborately decorated box that the Israelites used to symbolize God's presence among them. It contained, among other things, the tablets of the Law given by God to Moses. The Ark reminded the Israelites of God's Law and helped them obey it.

Ascension
The return of the Risen Christ in glory to his Father, to the world of the divine.

avarice
An excessive passion for wealth and power. It makes a god out of possessions. One of the seven capital sins.

B

Baptism
The sacrament celebrating birth into new life in Christ. The sacrament in which we are joined to Jesus Christ, become members of the Church, and are reborn as God's children. We receive the gift of the Holy Spirit, and original sin and our personal sins are forgiven.

beatific vision
Seeing God face-to-face in heavenly glory.

Beatitudes
Part of the Sermon on the Mount. The statements in the Gospel that begin with the phrase "Blessed are . . ." that describe the happiness of those who keep their life focused and centered on God. The sayings or teachings of Jesus that describe the qualities and actions of people blessed by God. The word *beatitude* means "blessing" or "happiness."

Bible (Sacred Scripture)
The collection of all the writings God has inspired human authors to write in his name.

Blessed Sacrament
The Eucharist reserved in the tabernacle.

Body of Christ
An image for the Church used by Paul the Apostle that teaches that all the members of the Church are one in Christ, the Head of the Church, and that all members have a unique and important work in the Church.

C

calumny
The making of true but damaging statements about another person's reputation or honor.

capital sins
Sins that are at the root of other sins—pride, avarice, envy, anger, gluttony, lust, and sloth.

chastity
The virtue that guides us in expressing our sexuality properly according to our state in life.

Christian morality
The way of living for people who have been joined to Christ in Baptism.

Church
The word *church* means "convocation, those called together." The Church is the sacrament of salvation—the sign and instrument of our reconciliation and communion with God and one another. The Body of Christ; the people God the Father has called together in Jesus Christ through the power of the Holy Spirit.

common good
The ultimate good each and every member of society has been created to achieve.

Communion of Saints
All the faithful followers of Jesus, both the living and the dead. The communion of holy things and holy people that makes up the Church.

concupiscence
The inclination to sin.

Confirmation
The sacrament that completes Baptism and that celebrates the special gift of the Holy Spirit.

conscience
The gift of God that is part of every human being that helps us judge right from wrong.

conversion
A renewal of our friendship with God and the Church; turning our hearts back to God's love and away from choices that weaken our friendship with God.

Covenant
The solemn agreement of fidelity that God and the People of God freely entered into, which was renewed in Christ, the new and everlasting Covenant.

covet
To want or desire what belongs to someone else; wrongfully treasuring another person's possessions, abilities, talents, friends, achievements, and so on.

D

Decalogue
The Ten Commandments.

deposit of faith
The source of faith that is drawn from to pass on God's Revelation to us; it is the unity of Scripture and Tradition.

detraction
The unjust revealing to a third party of someone else's faults or feelings.

direct abortion
The intentional killing of a child conceived but not yet born; that is, an unborn child who is still living in the mother's womb.

disciple
The follower of a teacher. In Christianity, a follower of Jesus; one who places total, unconditional trust in God the Father, as Jesus did—and in no one and nothing else.

divine Providence
God's caring love for us. The attribute of God that his almighty power and caring love is always with us.

Glossary

dogma of faith
A truth taught by the Church as revealed by God.

E

envy
The state of feeling angry or saddened that other people have something we do not have. Envy is one of the capital sins.

Eucharist
The sacrament in which we share in the Paschal Mystery of Christ and receive the Body and Blood of Christ, who is truly present under the appearances of bread and wine. The word *eucharist* is from a Greek word meaning "thanksgiving" or "gratitude."

euthanasia
The direct killing of a person who is suffering from a long-term or even terminal illness.

Evangelists
Inspired writers of the Gospel: Matthew, Mark, Luke, and John.

evangelize
To proclaim the Gospel.

Exodus
The journey of the Israelites out of slavery in Egypt to freedom under the leadership of Moses. Under the leadership of Moses the Israelites, or Hebrews as they were known in Egypt, went to the new homeland God promised them.

F-G

faith
The gift of God's invitation to us to believe and trust in him; it is also the power God gives us to respond to his invitation.

free will
The ability to recognize God as part of our lives and to choose to center our lives around him. The power to choose between good and evil.

gossip
Revealing personal or sensational facts about another person to harm them or to gain popularity for oneself.

grace
The gift of our sharing in God's life.

greed
The unchecked desire to have more and more things; wanting more and more things than we really need.

H

heresies
Religious opinions contrary to the teachings of the Apostles and the Church community.

holiness
Living our life in Christ; the characteristic of a person who is in right relationship with God. Holiness refers to God's presence with us and our faithfulness to God.

Holy Orders
The sacrament of the Church that consecrates baptized men as bishops, priests, or deacons to serve the whole Church in the name and person of Christ by teaching, divine worship, and governing the Church as Jesus did.

Holy Spirit
The third divine Person of the Holy Trinity sent to us by the Father in the name of his Son, Jesus.

Holy Trinity
The mystery of one God in three Persons—God the Father, God the Son, God the Holy Spirit.

I-J-K-L

icons
Pictures or images of Christ, Mary, a saint, or an angel.

idol
A false god; anything that takes the place of God in our lives.

intellect
The power to know God, ourselves, and others; the power to reflect on how God is part of our lives.

Jerusalem
The political and religious center of the Israelite people.

justification
The gift of new life in Christ that we receive at Baptism through sanctifying grace.

liturgical year
The cycle of seasons and feasts that make up the Church's year of worship.

liturgy
The Church's worship of God.

Lord's Prayer
The Our Father, the prayer that Jesus our Lord gave to the disciples and to the Church.

love
The greatest of all the gifts of the Holy Spirit.

Lumen Gentium
The Latin title meaning "Light of the Nations" for the document called *Dogmatic Constitution on the Church*, promulgated at the Second Vatican Council in 1964.

lying
Intentionally deceiving another person by deliberately saying what is false.

M

martyrs
Heroic figures who give their lives for their faith in Christ.

Matrimony
The sacrament of the Church that consecrates a baptized man and a baptized woman in a lifelong bond of faithful love as a living sign of Christ's love for the Church.

merit
To be worthy of or deserve.

moral virtues
Prudence, justice, fortitude, and temperance. They are also called the cardinal virtues.

morality
The term that describes the way we have been created to live. A means of evaluating whether our actions are good or evil; a way of judging whether our actions lead us to God or away from God.

mortal sin
Knowingly and willingly choosing to do something that is gravely contrary to God's Law; a serious, deliberate failure in our love and respect for God, our neighbor, creation, and ourselves; mortal sin completely kills the life of grace within us.

N-O

natural law
The foundation of moral life for everyone; the original sense of right and wrong that is part of our very being. It enables us by human reason to know good and evil.

obedience
The respectful listening and trusting response to a person who has authority over us and asks us to do something that is in accordance with God's Law or a just civil law.

order
The office in which one has a sacred duty to serve the Church. When a baptized man receives the sacrament of Holy Orders, he becomes a member of the order of bishop, priest, or deacon.

P-Q

Paschal Mystery
The saving events of the Passion, death, Resurrection, and glorious Ascension of Jesus Christ; the passing over of Jesus from death into a new and glorious life; the name we give to God's plan of saving us in Jesus Christ.

Pharisees
A lay sect within Judaism whose members have dedicated their lives to the strict keeping of the Jewish law found in the Torah.

precept
A rule or principle that imposes a particular standard of conduct or behavior on people.

R

rabbi
A teacher of the Law.

rash judgment
Rushing to judge another person's moral standing without sufficient reason or evidence.

Reconciliation
The sacrament through which we receive forgiveness of sins by the sincere confessing of our sins to a priest to whom the power to forgive sins has been given by the authority of the Church.

reparation
The action that must be taken to repair the damage done if we cause injustice to another.

reverence
The attitude of awe, profound respect, and love.

S

sacramentals
Sacred signs instituted by the Church. They include certain objects and blessings and prayers that prepare us to participate in the sacraments and make us aware of and help us respond to God's loving presence in our lives.

sacraments
Effective signs of grace, instituted by Christ and entrusted to the Church, by which divine life is shared with us; the seven main liturgical actions of the Church.

Sacraments at the Service of Communion
Holy Orders and Matrimony.

Sacraments of Christian Initiation
Baptism, Confirmation, and Eucharist.

Sacraments of Healing
Anointing of the Sick and Reconciliation (or Penance).

sanctification
The work of the Holy Spirit that unites us by faith and Baptism to the Passion and Resurrection of Christ. We become sharers of God's life through the work of the Holy Spirit.

sanctifying grace
God sharing his life and love with us; the gift of God's life and love that makes us holy; living in communion with the Holy Trinity.

sin
Freely and knowingly doing or saying what we know is against God's Law. Sin sets itself against God's love for us and turns our hearts away from God's love.

slander
Making false and damaging statements about another person's reputation or honor.

social sin
Individuals cooperating with one another and working against human life and human rights; we take part in social sin (1) when we participate directly and freely in another person's or group's sin; (2) when we order, advise, praise, or approve another person's or group's sinful acts; (3) when we fail to appropriately disclose or hinder another person's or group's sin when we can do so; (4) when we protect those who sin.

society
A group of people distinct from other groups and sharing a common culture, common interests, and common activities.

soul
The spiritual part of who we are that is immortal and never dies; our innermost being; that which bears the imprint of the image of God.

stewardship
The managing and caring for the property of another person. We are called to be stewards of God's creation.

subsidiarity
The principle that states that people have the right to self govern, that larger units of society have a responsibility to support and help coordinate the workings of the smaller units, and that smaller units must be allowed to do what they can for themselves when they are able to do so.

T

temptation
Everything that tries to move us to do or say something we know is wrong or from doing something good we know we can and should do; all that moves us away from living holy lives.

theological virtues
Faith, hope, and charity—strengths or habits that God gives us to help us attain holiness.

Torah
The Law of God revealed to Moses, which is found in the first five books of the Old Testament.

U-V-W-X-Y-Z

venial sin
A sin less serious than a mortal sin. It weakens our love for God and for one another.

virtue
Spiritual power or habit or behavior that helps us do what is right and avoid what is wrong.

worship
To honor and respect God above all else.

Index

Cover design: Kristy Howard
Cover illustration: Amy Freeman

CPSIA information can be obtained
at www.ICGtesting.com
Printed in the USA
LVHW021043051022
729895LV00005B/20